Over the Brink and Back

Over the Brink and Back

An inspiring tale of a remarkable recovery from a hugely challenging, life-threatening accident.

By Peter Rowlands

With contributions by:

Val Rowlands (Mum)

Anna (sister)

Andy (friend's father)

Rachel (physiotherapist)

Published in Great Britain 2022 by Pesda Press
Tan y Coed Canol
Ceunant
Caernarfon
Gwynedd
LL55 4RN

Copyright © 2022 Peter Rowlands

ISBN 9781906095901

Printed and bound in Poland, lfbookservices.co.uk

Dedication

I hope this piece serves as a reminder to all that we are stronger, more courageous and resilient when we are part of a family. I dedicate these words to my family.

Introduction

Many of us who participate in adventure sports have wondered: *"What if the worst really happened? What if everything I have held so dear were to be taken away in the blink of an eye: my way of living, my job, my social life ... everything?!"*

Photographic Acknowledgements

ix

About the Author

Peter Rowlands lived a life packed full of adventure. As a climber, mountaineer, skier, surfer and kayaker he constantly drove himself to the limit and lived life to the full.

Pete combined his passion for mountaineering with his career, and in 2010 qualified as a professional (IFMGA) Mountain Guide.

In 2013 he was caught in an avalanche which swept him over a cliff. Despite falling 140 metres and suffering serious brain injuries he survived. His prognosis was that in time he might be able to communicate by blinking.

Nine years later he has made a remarkable recovery and though sheer determination recovered his fitness levels. Pete does have speech problems and an odd gait but he has gone on to find new challenges. He has recently cycled the equivalent distance to once around the equator and continues to live life to the full.

Contents

Over the Brink and Back

April 2013 Austria

Kühtai – I always love being in Kühtai. Between December and April, it became my home from home. Sitting high above the Inn Valley and the city of Innsbruck, Kühtai nestles in a col overlooking the Tyrol region of the European Alps. It was my own little corner of paradise. In the village centre, bars, clubs and restaurants spill out, contributing to the alpine ambience. The tranquillity of the high Alps prevails, yet metres away, bright neon meets the jagged horizon.

According to friends and colleagues (it is highly unlikely that I'll ever recall this) I was, as per usual, heading to the Dortmunder Hütte, a roadside refuge owned by the Austrian Alpine Club. Its accommodation is basic but its proximity to great ski mountaineering more than compensates. I absolutely loved it there. We troughed a meal, washed it down with a full-bodied red and retired for an early night.

The next day saw us making our way up the Niedertal Valley to the Martin Bush Hut. In the clear, alpine morning, the group made good progress. Suddenly, above us, we heard a sharp retort, like the crack of an exploding artillery shell. A huge wall of heavy, wet snow, approximately one hundred metres across, weighing over a thousand tonnes and capable of demolishing a large house, accelerated down the slope towards us. I had just enough time to shout a warning to my companions before the avalanche engulfed me and carried me over the edge of a cliff ...

1986 Stockport – Learning the Ropes

I hated school. I wasn't academic and the only sport I excelled at was cross-country running. I didn't enjoy any of the team sports and have always harboured a dislike for football. If I'm ever in a park and a football accidentally comes over, I'll still always return it by hand. I considered school a massive inconvenience; it merely filled up my time. There was a brief attempt to ascertain whether I had any musical ability. I was very excited when the school music teacher said that I *"showed real natural talent and ability for playing the trombone"*. My sisters still love to remind me that they believed it was only because I had exceptionally long arms for my age but musically, it transpired that I was about as much use as a chocolate tea pot!

Everything changed at the grand old age of eight when my dad suggested we should go and climb Snowdon. In my mind's eye I imagined this climb would take several days, probably involving several camps and fixed ropes. It would not be dissimilar in profile to Springfield's 'Murderhorn', the fictitious, highest mountain in Springfield conquered by Grampa Simpson.

Leaving our car at the Pen-y-Pass hostel, we climbed over Y Lliwedd and then up onto the summit of Snowdon. I still remember standing on the summit and squinting at the Irish Sea, St. George's Channel and a very distant Ireland. That was my first experience of adventure. From that day on Dad and I had a lads' weekend in the Lake District, Snowdonia or Scotland every month. Those weekends meant the world to me, punctuating an otherwise seemingly monotonous existence.

However, my thirst for adventure couldn't be quenched by one weekend a month, so my mate and I decided to try our hand at rock climbing. At the age of eight we made the first and probably only ascent of Disley Quarry. We were both in the local Cub pack which used the same building as the Scout troop. One evening I took it upon myself to liberate a figure of eight from the storeroom. We clubbed what cash we had together and visited our local timber yard, purchasing 20 metres of polypropylene rope and a maillon rapide (a stainless steel industrial shackle). We managed to convince ourselves it was a proper karabiner but just a bit heavier!

With this incredibly basic assortment of kit and a distinct absence of knowledge, we were both ready for our epic ascent. Disley Quarry is a truly esoteric gem. The main wall boasts eight metres of 70° shale. The rope was tied around my waist, running around a small sapling at the top with my mate hanging on to the other end for grim death. I was ready to set forth into the vertical arena. Actually, to be totally honest, it was a short, moderately angled slab but I won't let objective facts ruin a boy's story. Several nights a week we pedaled our BMX bikes off into the sunset in search of adventure, and to avoid being sent to Mr Thompson's football club.

Climbing and mountaineering began to rule my life, giving me purpose and direction. I teamed up with two other boys, Robin and Simon Howarth who were family friends. As a threesome we served a proper, old-school 'gritstone apprenticeship'. Living on the edge of the Peak District and being able to pedal our bikes to most crags, our eyes were quickly opened to the quality and diversity of rock that Derbyshire has to offer. Our bikes could regularly be found at the bottom of Hobson Moor, Windgather Rocks, New Mills Torrs, Stanage Edge, Chee Dale and Millstone, to name but a few.

One Spring Saturday, our trio were spending the afternoon at Windgather Rocks. Perched high on a ridgeline, outside Buxton, its south westerly aspect catches the afternoon sun and enjoys far reaching views over the Cheshire plain to North Wales. A fellow climber stopped and engaged us in conversation. I thought that as he had a beard, he must be very knowledgeable. He had just founded a local climbing club called the Innominata Mountain Club and suggested we went along. From then on, every Tuesday evening and one day at a weekend, we'd climb locally and once a month we'd head to Wales or the Lake District. The Innominata gave me a sound grounding in, and appreciation of, climbing and mountaineering. In 1992 a fellow Innominata member instigated the building of a climbing wall; Rope Race, at Goyt Mill, all of two miles from my home. I knocked on the door of Rope Race, aged just 13, and politely asked if there were any chance of a job (a successful ploy). I was invited in and given a quick tour of their progress. The name Rope Race comes from the huge, steam engine it once housed. Via a system of pulleys and belts it provided power for each of the textile producing floors in the Goyt Mill; a perfect building for a climbing wall. I was bursting with excitement. A brilliant climbing wall was quickly taking shape near my house. Up to this point, I'd sometimes been to The Foundry in Sheffield and the wall at Glossop Leisure Centre. Now, climbing had become a way of life. I had the opportunity to climb every day and I did! I climbed or ran in every spare moment I had. The impact on my academic studies was all too obvious but it did mean, that by the age of 14, I was throwing myself at numerous E5s, and even getting up a few.

One evening, I was enjoying the evening sun while climbing Parker's Eliminate at Hobson Moor Quarry when I noticed two strong-looking lads, one with a blond ponytail and the other with short-cropped, brown hair, bouldering on the adjacent quarry wall. The ability of the former to keep his cool whilst soloing some of the most difficult terrain was quickly apparent with his solo ascent of Doug; a mind-bendingly hard E8 7a at the Roaches. Sam Whittaker, Steve Fisher, Paul Higginson and I were destined to spend the next seven years climbing and growing up together. The fourth member of what would become our quartet, was a former competitive gymnast, turned plumber, whose strength was legendary.

I was obsessed by climbing and anything to do with mountaineering. At school we were asked to do a presentation on a subject of our choice. So, along with my trusty old Stubai mountaineering axe (donated by my dad), Grivel walking crampons and fibreglass Joe Brown helmet, I caught the school bus and lectured my friends on the vertical world. That day, I started my apprenticeship in perhaps the most underrated skill a climber can possess, the art of telling a great story. It went so well that I was asked to speak at a Spoken English evening for the school parents. I was simultaneously reading Sweep Search by Hamish MacInnes. What a book, full of amazing adventure and altruism! That book definitely sowed the seeds for my involvement with the local mountain rescue team in years to come.

I seized the opportunity and, at the end of the lecture, had a quick whip round for the Glen Coe Mountain Rescue Team. I thought I was the bee's knees when I sent a check for several hundred pounds to Hamish MacInnes. A few months later I was on my way to Fort William with the Innominata Mountaineering Club and asked if I could stop in Glencoe and say hello to an acquaintance. A hushed silence fell over the other group members when we called in at Hamish's house and I was met with a big *"Hello mate, you've got bonny weather for the week!"*

By this point I'd accrued five years of climbing experience in Derbyshire, Wales and the Lake District but the scale of Scotland was other-worldly. I'd spent my youth with Dad climbing on the Idwal Slabs, the East face of Tryfan, Shepherd's Crag and Cwm Silyn so I'd already developed a functional level of competence and fitness. It has to be said that, at that stage, a good deal of my climbing was done alone on my training board in my Gran's garage. I was unquestionably the strongest and most technically gifted climber in the whole garage, if not Fairacres Road!

We'd come to Scotland to climb Ben Nevis via the Càrn Mòr Dearg Arête. It really was two for the price of one – two Munros in one sustained outing. As we snaked up Càrn Mòr Dearg Arête to Ben Nevis, Scotland really was everything and more than we had dreamt of. The route proved to be a long but very rewarding day in the mountains. The climbing felt engaging but at no point hard and the arête provided a magnificent view of the Ben's north face. Several hours later we stood aloft on Ben Nevis's summit, enjoying far-reaching views of The Great Glen and Skye.

I was preparing for my GCSEs, so must have been about 16 years old, when a friend at the climbing club said he could arrange for us to be mock students on an MIA (Mountain Instructor Award) assessment at Plas y Brenin, the National Mountain Centre in North Wales. Well, it sounded like a good day out, so off we went. We spent a very wet but enjoyable day on the Gribin Facet. Libby Peter, instructor / assessor, was looking on while I soaked up the view and the rain. It's seldom one can pinpoint a particular, definitive moment in one's life that influences its future path but there, in the rain, looking down the Ogwen Valley, my life's direction became clear – to work in the mountains.

Right then, I thought, I'll need some real experience. That week I bumped into a guy putting up a sign at the climbing wall reading *"winter climbing partner wanted"*. I explained that I had absolutely no winter climbing experience but was keen to learn, so most Fridays that winter, after school lessons had finished, we'd take off for Scotland. I didn't have much spare cash, so climbed in an old pair of ski salopettes, a Buffalo windshirt and a pair of Koflach Viva Soft boots I'd managed to acquire. On my head I had my old fibreglass Joe Brown helmet. My ice axes were Cassin Extremes with traditional picks and I wore Camp, strap-up crampons. Looking like I'd just been to a charity shop for blind climbers and having no knowledge other than climbing E4 / 5 on rock, I tied in and set off, hoping for the best. I had to rely exclusively on finding rock anchors as I couldn't afford ice screws.

As a slightly geeky, poorly-equipped rock climber, I climbed many routes and learned a lot that winter. I managed to find my way up Point Five Gully, Vanishing Gully, Castle Gully, Comb Gully, Green Gully and Tower Ridge on Ben Nevis, Pygmy Ridge in the Cairngorms and many more. We had a glorious week in the CIC hut, Ben Nevis, ticking off one or two classics every day. We were sharing the hut with Godefroy Perroux, a Mountain Guide, and his client. He made us tasty crêpes every night and recounted tales of alpine north faces, brutal storms and huge avalanches. My ears pricked up. The Alps sounded like a place of true adventure!

I knew I couldn't climb every day for the rest of my life, but maybe I could surf too. In fact, the greatest threat to my love of mountains and the vertical world was the ocean. Skiing fresh, champagne powder is amazing but not as amazing as surfing. It was too obvious an interest not to pursue. Agility, speed, balance, timing and experience all come together in an incredible crescendo that propels the surfer to an entirely new level of experience. Either that or you come brutally close to drowning. Both are hallmarks of a great session. Like climbing, it is an utterly addictive pursuit.

My first experience of surfing was as a young teenager during a family holiday to the Algarve in Portugal. Near Cape St. Vincent is Beliche beach. This beach is preferred by locals and has a notoriously strong rip current, so an obvious choice for me to repeatedly nearly drown and generally get in the way. Not having any idea about beach safety, I paddled straight into a rip and was quickly transported out to sea. In hindsight it was like taking a total novice climber to the North Face of the Eiger.

The wall and my new-found, second passion of surfing, placed a great strain on my academic studies. I was either at a crag somewhere in Derbyshire, up a mountain, winter climbing in Scotland, or on the beach in Wales but there are far worse obsessions to have as a teenager. I recently saw a lecture by the Cumbrian fell runner Billy Blandford. He believes those years between 6-18 are critical, in that, if you develop a good level of fitness in these years, you have it for life.

Over the Brink and Back

1995 Stockport – Decisions

I completed my GCSEs and then enjoyed a beautiful, long, hot summer's climbing. The 'fab four' took trips to Fontainebleau, Snowdonia and the Lake District. It seemed like climbing and the summer would last forever. But of course, they didn't.

I had no idea how to play the next few years. All I knew was that I wanted to climb. I enlisted on a sports science course at a local college. This experience came as a shock, as the last five years had been spent at a tiny grammar school. In my entire school there were only 150 students. Suddenly, I was surrounded by nearly a thousand other characters. Many of these were already performing at both regional and national level in their chosen sports. We formed a motley crew of basketball, rugby and lacrosse players, cyclists, swimmers, footballers, gymnasts … and me.

One of my fellow students was a huge basketball player. He disappeared with his friends for an hour every lunchtime. He must have gone somewhere very entertaining as he was always smiling on his return, if also a little lethargic. One afternoon we were conducting a practical session on VO2max. On a static bike we had to work to exhaustion, while wearing an air supply that monitored our oxygen consumption. When it was my turn, I noticed that the regulator appeared to be malfunctioning. I really had to fight to get a breath. What I should have done was draw the attention of the lecturer to the issue. What I actually did was to hand the apparatus on to my giddy, lethargic colleague and subsequently watched the 'fireworks'. He sprinted for about two minutes on the bike, then collapsed dragging all the equipment off the work surface and knocking the static bike over. I picked him up, immediately pulled the mask off his face and said *"Easy mate, I fear you've over-egged the pudding a little."*

The great thing about going to college was the work experience module. I had to choose from a long list of sports coaches and leisure centres, none of which took my fancy. I never really wanted to be a Gordon Brittas type. In the end I opted to organise my own work experience. I arranged a two-week period at Derbyshire County Council's outdoor education centre, White Hall. I was placed under the direction of Rory Gregory, a friendly member of the IFMGA (International Federation of Mountain Guides Associations), who like me, was a habitual climber. It was only a month after I'd met a Guide on Ben Nevis and first understood what a Guide is. Throughout my teenage years I was desperate to be a Royal Marine. My climbing friends started calling me *"Marine"*, although they quickly amended it to *"Maurine"* when I changed my mind. My IFMGA men-

14

tor pointed out that there was another way to work in the mountains *"and you won't run the risk of getting shot this way"*.

It was definitely a sports science course. Science with a capital S. Within a few weeks of starting, we sat a human biology exam. Twenty-six years on, I can still remember my consternation as I opened the paper. One question read as follows, *"What is the name of the clotting agent found in the blood stream?"* Wow, hang on ... I thought. That's a bit of a swerve ball. I'm 16, I've just left school. I raised my hand but the exam invigilator was busy doing her own work. A loud cough caught her attention and I asked to be excused to visit the bathroom. She nodded and carried on with her work.

Right, I thought. If you can't be bothered to supervise a proper exam, I can't be bothered being a proper candidate. I jumped in the lift and went down two floors to the college library. Under 'Human Biology' I immediately found the answer, fibrinogen, and I seem to remember that it is a protein. I retraced my steps without problem and completed the examination. When the class was reviewing the paper, I was complimented on my knowledge. I've got many faults, but modesty has never been one of them. I agreed that my knowledge regarding the subject was extensive!

It was then pointed out that the course carried equivalent UCAS points to A levels in PE, Biology and Chemistry. Ok, I thought, I really need to up my game if I'm going to pass this course, I need a plan.

You must remember this was 1996. The internet was in its infancy and smart watches wouldn't be invented for another twenty years. The plan was simple but effective; arrive at the exam early and bag a seat near the window, as far away from the invigilator as possible, wear combat pants with generous A5 sized pockets on the thighs. Make extensive notes but always on cardboard to reduce any rustle, find a trustworthy tutor who was happy to talk me through the biomechanics and chemistry course work.

My plan worked well and gained me access to a BSc course!

1998 Ambleside – University

I knew I wanted to obtain a university degree but wasn't sure in which subject. Let me rephrase that. I wanted to hang out with like-minded people for 3 years; go climbing, mountaineering and kayaking. If I could achieve that under the auspices of academia and emerge a graduate, fantastic. The only course that I considered was a BSc in Outdoor Studies at St. Martin's College, University of Cumbria, Ambleside. The course consisted of 60% Ecology and 40% Outdoor Education. I tried to sign up for the distance learning option, choosing to base myself in Chamonix, but sadly (although not surprisingly) I discovered that this was not an option.

Andy:

My wife, Ann, and I are delivering our son, Ian, to university to commence a BSc in Outdoor Studies. He is assigned to a hall of residence and allotted a room number – we knock and walk in. There are two single beds in the pleasantly appointed room. From the nearest bed an impressively tall, widely grinning, young man unfolds himself, proffering a large and friendly hand "Hi, I'm Pete". And so it began.

The campus was situated right at the foot of the Fairfield Horseshoe. After our initial spell in halls of residence, a group of three other lads, Ian and I took lodgings in a battered, cold, damp and smelly house in Ambleside. To truly make this residence our own, we decided we must first name the house and have a suitable slate sign commissioned. Inspiration wasn't far away. A stone's throw up the road lay Dove Cottage, home to William Wordsworth. Now, 'thwaite' (a piece of wild land cleared or reclaimed for cultivation) is commonly used in Cumbrian place names. Could I dream up a name that perhaps utilized 'thwaite' and represented the house mantra and values? We agreed upon 'Pornthwaite'!

I went to university when I was 19. At that point, I'd developed a lot of ability in many different disciplines but was simply too young to have much experience. In sports other than climbing, I represented a level of incompetence. The kayakers at university took me under their wing and I followed them down some epically-steep, Cumbrian becks. We also kayaked in Scotland, France and Spain. Kayaking requires a different mindset than that required for climbing. For a climber in the early 90s, power and strength were regarded as key. The adage I lived by was coined by Ben Moon, a climber of that time: *"Technique is no substitute for power"*. Climbing was slow, considered and careful. The brain is bombarded by stimuli from proprioceptors as you commit to each move. On the contrary, kayaking seemed fast and 'in your face'. Climbing affords you time to respond to the stimuli. Kayaking demands rapid, forward planning before an event occurs and immediate responses to the constantly changing environment.

What you don't know, you don't know. As a group of young, keen kayakers, we would throw ourselves down anything. Epic rescues, terrible beatings and lengthy swims were normality. One midweek night, we were all drinking in Ambleside's Golden Rule pub until last orders. Someone then suggested we should go kayaking. So, semi-drunk and in the pitch black, we kayaked the River Leven, four miles of grade 4. Our disregard for safety was appalling. Oh the folly of youth! I was 19 at the time and felt totally indestructible. The stage was set for a horrendous accident.

One wet, autumnal day we drove over to the far side of Kendal to make a descent of the River Kent. It had been raining for days and the river had already broken its banks. Several cans of Red Bull and half an hour of ear-bleed inducing techno later we were all itching to get on the water. The river was alive and the flow was fast and rowdy, but we enjoyed success on several rapids graded 4+. As the river enters Kendal it becomes canalised and greatly loses its power and speed. I sat back and congratulated the others on another brilliant descent.

Suddenly a horizon line appeared, and then a deep, throaty rumbling became audible. Quickly, we all shifted mental gear again. Perhaps we hadn't finished? We could now see a group of kayakers on the riverbank trying desperately to gain our attention. They were all pointing at the horizon line and waving desperately. I quickly assessed our options. The river was still canalised with smooth 10-foot walls on either side. The rumbling got steadily louder and a hazy spray now sat over the horizon line.

Unwittingly, we had committed ourselves to a 'death weir'. The only option now was speed. I engaged hyper-drive and paddled as hard as I possibly could. The deep roar of the weir was now deafening. With total luck I carried enough speed over the lip to clear the boil line and stopped paddling. I didn't realise at the time, but I'd started to get sucked back into the weir. Once again, I dropped a gear and paddled to safety.

My paddling friend wasn't so lucky. The recirculating current sucked him back into the weir's guts and gave him a furious beating. He described lifting his arms above his head and feeling the concrete of an overhanging weir. He was there for minutes being recirculated and recirculated. Eventually he surfaced for a split second. Just long enough for a line to be thrown to him.

That day we had come within a hair's breadth of drowning. My mate lay gasping on the riverbank. What you don't know, you don't know – and some lessons are hard learnt!

As well as kayaking in Cumbria and Yorkshire we occasionally drove north, ate deep fried pizza, drank 80 Shilling and hurled ourselves down some epic Scottish ditches. The River Etive is a trade route for kayakers. I will never forget the feeling of weightlessness as

I emerged from a constricted dogleg, and found myself looking straight down a five-metre waterfall.

We'd done some kayaking road trip preparation and researched a spot called the Falls of Lora, near Oban. We'd all drooled over pictures of glassy, clean, green waves, beautiful scenery and blue skies. The Falls of Lora are created by the tide flooding a sea loch, through a narrow opening. When the tide ebbs, the seaward side drops faster than the loch can drain. This results in a strong, fast-flowing channel of water. At its narrowest point the fast-flowing stream flows over a reef. This results in an abundance of standing waves, whirlpools and confused water.

We timed our trip to coincide with a spring tide. It was massive. I got on for an epic, white-knuckle ride and then disappeared backwards into a whirlpool. The experience stands alone as the single most violent beating of my life. I feared my head would be spun off my body. I'm sure the only reason I survived was because I stayed in my kayak and Eskimo rolled when I reached the surface. My kayak had a capacity in the region of 186 litres and I went very deep. Without my kayak, I would have been sent to Davy Jones' locker!

As it was, I had a battered ego and a huge smile across my face when I was finally reunited with dry land.

It wasn't until university that I also found an ingenious system for combining revision and surfing; write some revision notes, seal them into a plastic bag then tape them onto my board. Whilst sitting in the line-up, waiting for the next set, I'd glance down and read, *"carbon, nitrogen, oxygen, sulphur, phosphorus, and water are the macro nutrients that are recycled"*.

One dreary, autumnal day, three of us were walking down Keswick high street in the cold, November rain when, in all honesty, our combined attention was diverted to the staff in the travel agency by a particularly beautiful lady. Collectively we smiled, then one of us suggested we should go in. Within 15 minutes we'd bought a flight, departing the next morning, to spend the week surfing in Fuerteventura. We didn't have two pennies to rub together. We camped on the beach for a week and surfed from dawn till dusk every day.

The course was anything but a conventional university experience. After a few hours of study, we were actively encouraged to disappear into the mountains. My tutor, Terry Storry, was a Mountain Guide, a prolific climber and kayaker. With him, we skied in Alpe d'Huez and kayaked in Briançon. This course was pitched at the perfect level for my version of academia. Despite numerous climbing ground falls, snowboarding accidents and near drowning incidents, we all staggered over the finish line.

Andy:

Incredibly the lads graduated and were then to spend yet another few years climbing, skiing and adventuring, gaining suitable experience and qualifications before ending up with real jobs.

In retrospect, I had led a pretty wild youth. Through-out my later teens, I partied far too hard. A friend, Bruce, and I often undertook slightly bizarre adventures such as our night-time aid ascent of Thor's Cave in Derby-shire. We arrived in midwinter at Thor's Cave at 19:00. Armed with head torches and an assortment of climbing kit, we brachiated through the roof of the cave. For over six hours we pulled from old bolt to peg, following the miles and miles of tiny limestone passages as we caved deep under Derbyshire.

We could also regularly be found reaching for the lasers in the once famous Hacienda night club, Manchester. It was on one of these nights as a teenager that I made a slight, culinary faux pas. On arriving back at home at 03:00, I was hit with a bout of hunger. A quick glance in the fridge revealed the remains of last night's family meal - braised steak, my favourite! I warmed the portion and wolfed down the generous plateful. I'm no Michelin food critic but I have to speak the truth, it was notably below par and had a rubbery, gritty texture. It was the following morning when Mum enquired, *"Did you feed the dogs when you got in last night? I left a plate of Pedigree Chum in the fridge."* Nothing a generous gargle of mouth wash wouldn't solve!

In my early twenties with friends, we risked life and limb on innumerable alpine north faces, surfed giant, Atlantic swells in the South West, battled our way down steep rivers in North Wales and the Lake District and skied steep and, quite frankly, terrifying alpine couloirs.

23

Another pastime involved throwing ourselves off huge structures like the Menai Suspension Bridge. Our bridge-swinging epic above the Menai Straits necessitated attaching a rope in the middle of the bridge, then walking 40 metres beyond it before throwing ourselves into the abyss so we swung like pendulums under the span.

Now life would become a little less wild, if still fraught with risk, as I made progress towards my intended career.

February 2003 Plas y Brenin, North Wales

As a result of the counsel and recommendation of my IFMGA mentor, becoming a Mountain Guide seemed the obvious career path for me to follow. However, I had quickly realised that ability and experience were two completely different things. As a result of my 10-year commitment to climbing, I could pull exceptionally hard on very small holds and by my mid-teens I'd climbed a few Scottish winter classics. I was, however, keen to serve a full apprenticeship. The road I chose was long and arduous but, when completed, would assure a depth of experience.

After a summer and winter of climbing and skiing in the Alps, it was now time to further my progress towards my intended career by spending a year as an Assistant Instructor at Plas y Brenin. I was brimming with confidence regarding my personal ability, but I was on the very first rung of the ladder when it came to experience. The learning curve for a university graduate at Plas y Brenin was incredibly steep. As well as working in the mountains every day, we were asked to deliver a wide range of evening lectures, plan for the following day's teaching and prepare for the important Mountaineering

Instructor Award assessment. The lectures spanned a broad range of new topics including, the legal and moral responsibilities of a Mountain Leader, the flora and fauna of Snowdonia and the geology of the area. After the winter's hedonism in Chamonix, the new routine came as quite a shock, but we did manage the requisite work schedule and still find the time to climb after work most evenings.

Being in the mountains is very like being at sea. They are a setting for acts of true altruism. Before I joined the Mountain Rescue Team, while working at Plas y Brenin, I was enjoying a day off in the summer sunshine at Dinas Cromlach, Llanberis. I had just climbed the classic route, Cenotaph Corner and was eating my lunch on the ledges below, when I heard a loud bang and a scream from above. I took a spare rope and soloed the first pitch of an easy route called Spiral Stairs to investigate the source of the disturbance. A girl had fallen from the crux of Sabre Cut and hit the broad ledge system known as The Forest. A semi-conscious girl sobbed at the intense pain coming from her lumbar spine. I made her secure and then shouted down to my climbing partner to call the police and request a helicopter. Due to the mechanism of the injury and the risk of spinal damage I was keen she was taken to hospital as soon as possible, but she would need to be evacuated carefully, on a rigid stretcher. The girl was in real discomfort. I was trying to reassure her when we heard the distant rumble of an engine. I put my hand on her shoulder and said, *"Don't worry, it's here now. You'll soon be in hospital"*. A jet flew overhead and into the distance. I could sense her disappointment and agony. After another ten minutes a Sea King helicopter lumbered up the valley. The extraction and evacuation were wild, as we were on a tiny, sloping ledge. After receiving and securing the winchman we loaded her onto a stretcher. All together, the winchman and stretcher were winched up to the aircraft. They paused for a second and then disappeared. The melodic boom of its rotors grew distant. I visited the girl in Bangor hospital the following day. She had severely broken her back, but luckily not severed or damaged her spinal cord. The surgeon had said, *"If anyone had tried to move you, it would have been a totally different outcome."*

I often return to that thought. When I make a mistake and curse my actions, I console myself with that memory and think, that lady can only walk because, on that day, you were right and reacted quickly.

The year at Plas y Brenin saw me working alongside top climbing, mountaineering and kayaking coaches. It really was an apprenticeship for outdoor work. Possibly the most significant outcome was the reassurance that this was exactly the career path I wanted. The year also enabled me to gain my Mountaineering Instructor Award.

Over the Brink and Back

28

October 2003 USA

It was with some relief that we all successfully completed the year at Plas y Brenin, and then headed to the USA for a well-earned climbing holiday. We were driving from Las Vegas to the famous desert town of Moab when a state trooper pulled us over. With one hand resting on his firearm, he slowly sauntered up to the vehicle, which Dave Hollinger was driving. An officious looking sheriff complete with wide-brimmed hat, aviator shades and a neat moustache, indicated that the driver should roll the window down. I suppressed the urge to ask him if he had performed with the Village People and listened to his question:

"Sir you were travelling at exactly 94kmph. Can you tell me how much over the limit you were?"

Hang on, I thought, Dave's not Carol Vorderman. He'll run out of fingers and toes to count on!

The climbing was simply out of this world. We enjoyed several weeks of soaring towers, splitter cracks, desert views and autumn light. As usual, we completed the trip on a tight budget, renting one tiny motel room each night, then four of us piling in complete with camping mats and sleeping bags.

To this day Las Vegas is the only place where I've been defeated by a salad. I thought I'd ordered a salad not an allotment! However, the daily ritual of coffee, pancakes and climbing was just what we all needed.

High above the town of Moab sit The Three Penguins. It would seem that they are collectively gazing out towards the sun and distant horizon. They are in fact three sandstone towers that vaguely resemble penguins. The spot offers a beautiful setting for an afternoon's climbing, close to the car and the world-famous Delicate Arch.

Dave Hollinger, Martin Doyle and I had an afternoon there, opting for a butch looking, overhanging crack system. What to do with flared cracks was the question? I had served a fifteen-year gritstone apprenticeship, a medium that demands slow thoughtful movement. Being well out above my gear, in seemingly blank terrain, was my modus operandi. Butch, off-width cracks were totally alien. I cammed my knee deeply into the crack, relieving the weight from my arms, allowing me to place a very high hex. By now I had traversed around several roofs and the calls of encouragement from Dave and Martin were fading and growing ever more distant. I had now been doing battle with the corner system for half an hour. Lactic acid flooded my arms as the fight steadily ebbed away. At 6'5" tall with a positive ape index, reach has never been a problem. In a last ditch attempt, I threw a high lock into the crack directly above my head. It failed and moved; fatigue was now consuming me but suddenly, my failing fingers settled on the high hex I had just placed and gripped. I couldn't possibly do that, could I? I took a quick glance over my shoulder to ensure the lads couldn't see me, then pulled like a tractor on the hex.

The rest of the pitch was a steady 5.10 (E2 5c). And I soon arrived at the stance. Both Dave and Martin required assistance to overcome the crux. On arriving at the stance, they enquired, *"how on earth did you get up that? It was insane!"* *"A gritstone apprenticeship."* I replied. A gritstone apprenticeship and 'French free', I thought. My colleagues were both so impressed with my performance that day, that the story made it back across the Atlantic before I did and I received a hero's return. *"Oh, it was nothing."* I said modestly.

Some twenty years later when Dave Hollinger was recovering in hospital from a brutal skiing accident, I wrote to both lads and finally confessed: *"Erm lads, remember my legendary performance on the Penguins above Moab? ... Sorry, my ego got the better of me."*

I was more the end of a leg than legend!

Over the Brink and Back

January 2004 North Wales – Teaching

In my early twenties I had the enviable job of teaching Outdoor Education at a day and boarding school in North Wales. Part of the impressive building dates from the sixteenth century. It is Grade I listed and set in the beautiful grounds of a former manor house. Its appearance and setting are not dissimilar to Hogwarts, of Harry Potter fame. I guess that should have made me Hagrid. I was actually Chief Instructor and responsible for the daily deployment of my staff, with whom I took students skiing in France and Switzerland, surfing in Cornwall and diving in the Red Sea. Many of my students have subsequently been very successful in the great outdoors e.g. having worked at the National Mountain Centre, Scotland, represented Scotland in skiing, worked at the National White Water Centre, North Wales and qualified as Mountain Instructors.

At the time I lived in Llanberis, a forty-minute drive from the school, depending on the morning traffic. As staff briefing was 08:30, I would have to leave promptly at 07:45. In the summer months this was always quite an ask as, invariably, I'd climb every night after work, often staggering in long after 22:00.

One morning, I was running late and hurtling along the coast road, listening to fast and furious dance music in the vain hope it would wake me up. I arrived at work just in time, now driving slowly and cautiously up the long school drive.

The headmaster walked to work, up the drive, every morning and I knew I was likely to encounter him. Suddenly realising Airforce 1, my old Transit van, was still vibrating to the sounds of Faithless, I hurriedly changed channels to BBC Radio 4's Today programme. The reassuring tones of John Humphrys boomed out of my stereo just as I passed the head. He waved and enquired, *"and what's happening in the world today, Mr Rowlands?"* *"Well, apparently Maxi Jazz is still suffering from acute insomnia"* I replied under my breath (for the uninitiated, Maxi Jazz is the lead vocalist of the band Faithless and the track hurriedly obliterated from my stereo was Insomnia).

The job was perfect for my alpine climbing obsession. It afforded a predictable wage, and incredibly generous and frequent holidays. It meant that during the year I could enjoy four long months of alpine climbing, mountaineering and skiing. I never did the lads' holiday thing. That cringeworthy scene from The Inbetweeners when they all meet at the airport, in horrendously inappropriate T-shirts was never on my radar. That sort of behaviour is so much more dignified when disguised as an alpine climbing holiday. The final, summer term staff meeting occurred in the first week of July. I would drive straight from the meeting in my battered old Transit van and spend two months in or around the Alps, and return just in time for the next staff meeting in early September, always exhausted, emaciated and sun burnt. Although I lived on a shoe-string budget and either worked or climbed, I did manage to pack an amazing amount in.

During the winter months I tried to winter climb in Scotland every Monday and Tuesday (my days off). After a full day at work on Sunday, I'd jump into Airforce 1 and make the drive north. One Monday morning I'd arranged to climb with Blair Ffyfe. After 9 hours of drafty, noisy, slow, exhausting driving in Airforce 1, I finally arrived in Spean Bridge. Although Airforce 1 carried friends and I all over Europe to various mountains, cliffs, rivers and beaches, its absence of power steering, a small unreliable engine, multiple holes and a top speed of 75mph, made driving it an exhausting affair. Somewhat like piloting a Lancaster Bomber I would imagine. I treated myself to four hours of sleep in the back, until Blair was banging on my window at 05:30. *"We're off to Coire an Laoigh to try the modern classic, Blue Rinse, a mind-boggling, run out VII 7."*

It was a cold, crisp morning with absolutely perfect conditions. I made us both a coffee for the journey and bailed into his beat-up old Fiat Panda for the journey along the miles and miles of deserted Forestry Commission track. The route we had planned tackled a soaring arête. I hadn't thrown a winter tool for a good month, and the feeling of doing 0-60 in climbing grades was soon all too apparent. Within seconds, at 08:00 on a remote Scottish mountain I was, once again, climbing for my life. Blair was always the understated professional. In his broad Scottish accent, he'd say: *"Watch that, it's a wee bit thin"* which actually meant *"Good luck, it's desperate!"*

I climbed second on the top pitch. The crux of the climb traversed some wildly exposed, technically demanding and committing terrain. The climb was now as serious for the second as for the leader. The result of a fall for either of us would be a massive pendulum swing. On arriving at the summit, calm once again descended over us both. The race was over. Stopping occasionally to knock snow off our crampons, we started a long descent and headed directly to the Little Chef. We looked very out of place eating a huge fry up with all the other truckers, but welcomed the feed.

Blair was an avalanche forecaster and field observer for Lochaber. I never failed to pick his brains and ask him to quickly dig a pit revealing the different layers of snow. The strata revealed the recent climatic history, and the collection of snow crystals could be linked to each meteorological event that had battered the mountains. However, knowing that he was also an astrophysicist, I would sometimes try my very best to sound sincere and ask questions such as, *"So Blair, I'm a Libra, will the next one be a good month?"* My crow's feet always betrayed me as I tried not to laugh.

One Christmas, I had agreed with some friends to spend a month climbing and mountaineering in Scotland together, but the inclement weather seemed perpetual. For two weeks we did a grand tour of Torridon, the Northwest Highlands, the Cairngorms, Ben Nevis and Glen Coe. Each day we hoped for sub 60mph wind and a break in the clouds. It never came. The final straw was an adventurous plan to cross the Cairngorm plateau, spend a night in the Hutchinson Memorial Hut and climb the next day. I stand at 6'5". The sleeping area is about 5'5", a slab of stone. After no sleep we walked for 6 hours into the teeth of a blizzard, straight back to Airforce 1. Without missing a beat, we drove directly to the southern French Alps and spent two weeks climbing steep ice in La Grave.

I'd driven (piloted) Airforce 1 for thousands of miles when I returned to the UK, but I still had unfinished business with the Hutchinson Memorial Hut. Our original intention had been to throw ourselves at Càrn Etchachan, Route Major in the Cairngorm Massif, and what an appropriate name that was. The climb really is a remote undertaking. I was climbing with Kath Bromfield. Two years later we'd climb the North Face of the Eiger together with Stu McDonald, and the seriousness of this remote classic lent itself perfectly to forging that partnership. Route Major takes a very direct line on the crag. It was never really hard or technically demanding but always engaging. On arriving at a summit, thoughts naturally progress to after climb celebrations. However, the route off Càrn Etchachan then requires another four hours of what proved to be quite involved navigation as, once again, we battled across the plateau.

37

Whilst gainfully employed as a teacher in North Wales, with significant holidays at my disposal, I completed all the Mountain Training (UK) assessments (these included Single Pitch Award, Summer and Winter Mountain Leader assessments, Mountain Instructor Award and Certificate).

Now I was ready to complete the prerequisite experience required to be accepted on the IFMGA Mountain Guide training scheme. This experience included:

20 rock climbs of grade E1 5c and above

20 Scottish winter climbs of grade 5 or above

5 years summer experience

10 climbs of 1000+ metres and Très Difficile in grade

20 days of ski mountaineering from hut to hut

The IFMGA training, aspirant period and assessments would then follow. This route would ensure ability and experience in equal measure. Due to an absolute focus on my goal from my teenage years, I was to pass every assessment first time.

In my (very little) spare time, I also volunteered with the Llanberis Mountain Rescue Team. The team covered Snowdon and was in fact the busiest team in the country. I always tried my hardest to insert some humour into an otherwise stressful situation. One autumnal day I responded to a call from a couple of climbers who'd become 'off route' and disoriented, high on the flanks of Crib Goch. It was midweek, and I was by myself when I finally found the cold, sheepish pair. They started by apologising profusely. Trying to lighten the mood I replied, *"Lads, you've done me a real favour, she would have had me cutting the lawn. Let's get ourselves sorted and then have a quick pint in the Vaynol Arms."*

Over the Brink and Back

April 2004 France – Gaining Experience

Departing from Argentière and snaking through some of the most impressive mountain scenery in Western Europe; the Haute Route is a must for any ski mountaineer.

In 2003 along with three mates, Dave Evans, Dave Hollinger, and Stuart McAleese, I had the pleasure of attempting this multi-day, high level traverse. By now, I'd spent a winter skiing and partying in Chamonix (mainly partying) and had made ascents of numerous hard, alpine climbs. There is a well-known saying that states that 'prior planning and preparation, prevents poor performance'. You would like to think that an iconic, four / five-day, high mountain traverse would be treated with the respect it deserved and the usual ritual of poring over maps, checking and double checking our gear would have followed. The only fly in the ointment was that Chamonix is the Las Vegas of the mountains and, anyway, we were in our early twenties and alcohol supposedly thins the blood, aiding acclimatisation. We considered all these points and then headed into town.

Dave Evans and I pioneered a dance move that we've rolled out in numerous night clubs from Wales to the

South of France. We called it the 'assisted head spin'. It requires an audience, athletic participants and enough alcohol to fill a swimming pool. Neither of us are nearly cool enough to actually be able to breakdance, but we both score A for effort. One member of our dance crew drops onto their head and is supported by the other holding their feet. The breakdancer is then rotated at a very pedestrian pace, to mimic a head spin. In years to come I damaged my cervical spine in a climbing accident. On looking at the X-rays, the doctor quizzed me and asked, *"Other than this accident, can you think of any excess load to the area?"*. I suppressed a giggle and said, *"Ermm, no"*. During the same visit the doctor tested my nervous responses. He hit my right knee under the kneecap with a hammer. I jolted my left leg out. I don't need any encouragement!

We all staggered out of Dicks T-bar nightclub at 02:00, grabbed a few hours sleep in the back of Airforce 1 and were ready for the off. Feeling a little green around the gills we jumped on the Grand Montets cable car. At the mid station we quickly transferred to the top station cabin. The cabin catapults the skier to a lofty 3295m in a matter of minutes. From the raging music of a Chamonix night club, followed by the thronging masses of a busy ski area, you're suddenly immersed in nothingness and absolute silence. There's no noise more pleasing than the gentle hiss created by skis floating on fresh powder snow as you accelerate down the mountain side. A few gentle turns and we found our stride. Once again, the 'fab four' were loving it.

After a few hours we were assembled at the top of the first steep section, the Col de Chardonnay. By now our transitions were smooth and efficient. In a very short time, we'd put skis on our rucksacks, crampons on our feet and with ice axes in hand we started climbing down several hundred metres of steep narrow couloir. Suddenly came distant shouting from above, *"Attention!"*. Far above us a party had dislodged a dinner size plaque of bulletproof ice. We could hear its far-off hum as the projectile bore down on us. In such situations the mind frantically explores any possibility of cover. A few metres above me Dave Evans let out a shrill cry. The plaque had collided with his bare head. Stunned and knocked off balance he went through a motion like winding down a car window. Blood trickled down his forehead and into his eyes as we climbed down the final few metres. At the base of the steep section, I took my rucksack off and searched through the basic first aid provisions I had with me. Now, my medical knowledge was, and still is, basic. Add to that the fact that we were high on a mountain side, just out of the line of fire. I applied a bandage, wrapped around his head and under his chin. It successfully stemmed the blood loss but in retrospect he looked like a Passchendaele survivor. After lots of ranting and swearing we continued on our way to finish at the Trient mountain hut. Smelling like a brewery and with Dave resembling an Egyptian mummy we didn't perhaps represent the elite, mountaineer image we'd hoped for. However, we were en route, and sobriety had now returned to us all. Dave was complaining of a splitting headache, but I genuinely think that it was partly induced by tequila.

The next three days were eventless affairs, as all good trips in the mountains should be. The route really is something to behold. By night the buzz of busy mountain huts offered a warm, social dynamic to our journey, but by day the mountains seemed eerily quiet. The final day takes a long sweeping descent into Zermatt, directly under the North Face of the Matterhorn. Only a few years previously, Dave Hollinger had made a successful ascent of the North Face and talked us through the complex route. On arrival in Zermatt, we had already missed the final train. This set the scene for what is undoubtedly one of the greatest trans-alpine races ever undertaken. In years to come, it will be talked about in the same breath as Uli Steck's Eiger solo or Marco Pantani's ascent of Alp d'Huez in the 1995 Tour de France. It was the 'blue boots' versus the 'orange boots' hitching race back to Chamonix! Stuart and I were wearing Scarpa Denali, blue boots and the two Daves, Scarpa Laser, orange boots. Stuart and I were obviously far better looking, more approachable, sociable and more modest. We wasted no time at all and easily linked lifts and 'flew' back to Chamonix, faster than a photon. To rub salt in the wound, I rang the 'orange boots' team when we arrived in Chamonix. They were still stood roadside in Switzerland. With the promise of the purchase of a burger for my efforts, I jumped into Airforce 1 and drove over to Switzerland to end their hitching nightmare. So ended our first Haute Route experience. I have since guided the route multiple times, in a contrasting and thoroughly professional manner!

Over the Brink and Back

December 2004 – The Italian Job

As usual, Airforce 1, my trusty old chariot, carried my mate and myself across Europe to the Alps. We had agreed to team up with four other lads, one of whom had an orange, ex AA Transit, another had a red Transporter. I can date the trip, as I thought Dave Hollinger's new purchase of a gadget that turned cassette music into a short-wave radio frequency that could be played through your van stereo was amazing. The three of us could drive our vans in close formation and enjoy shared techno as we all tuned into the same frequency.

First stop on the lads' tour was Chamonix. Two of the lads were drowning their sorrows after being beaten back off the Croz Spur on the north face of the Grande Jorasses. As good and thoughtful friends, we joined them. In the next few days, we climbed steep ice in Cogne in the Aosta Valley and the days formed a predictable but agreeable pattern. Rise early, climb a brutally steep icefall then head back to Cogne village and celebrate with a hot chocolate. Repeat. We were all having a very enjoyable time and definitely a holiday. The next day we'd planned to rest our arms and do some skiing over at Gressoney.

I've used the proceedings of that day as a case study in avalanche lectures, innumerable times. We were staying in Epinel, just below Cogne. A two-hour drive from Gressoney. As we weren't going to be climbing, we sampled a bit too much of the local wine the night before. We arrived late in Gressoney and had no clear plan for the day. As we went up in the cable car, I noticed that there were raised remains of ski tracks everywhere. This was the biggest single clue. Skiers had compressed the snow under their skis. The remaining snow had blown away, smashing and damaging the interlocking fingers on the edges of the snow crystals, making the rafts of wind-blown snow less cohesive. These resulting rafts of snow are known as wind slab. They can be identified by a slightly dull, chalky appearance. A tell-tale squeak when compressed is heard and shooting cracks can often be sighted as a block fails. All that wind-blown snow had to go somewhere. In this instance, just where we were heading.

We skied a bit on-piste and a bit off-piste and finally decided to grab a coffee from a mountain refuge. We cut about twenty metres off the edge of the piste to traverse around the back of a café. There was a crack like a whip, and then the mountain was moving.

Four of the lads and I stepped off the front of the slide into the coffee queue. But Dougal Tavener was picked up and driven into the back wall of the café. He was very nearly catapulted through the kitchen window. The avalanche ran off into the valley and we ran back around the building to find Dougal partially buried against the building. He was screaming for help so our coffee would have to wait while we dug him out. It was a very close call. Luckily, we were able to reach Dougal in seconds and then made him buy the coffee!

The major learning outcome from this is: keep a weather-eye out for wind slab – whether you're off-piste by several kilometres, or several metres.

Over the Brink and Back

Spring 2005 The Alps

The secret to successful alpinism is not becoming entrenched in your plans. Having the ability to change your mind or your plan quickly, and seemingly without effort, is the difference between good and great. A skill Dave Evans and I demonstrated in 2005.

We had a huge list of objectives to try and complete during our spring ski touring, north face, alpine trip. As it turned out, the weather was terrible and constant storms battered the mountains. It wasn't for lack of trying but eventually we cut our losses. We still had 3 weeks of holiday left and were dammed if we were going to waste it. The decision was made to go to Céüse sport climbing instead. The one flaw was that we'd come on an alpine climbing and skiing holiday. We could throw some quick draws together and I had an old rope in the back of Airforce 1 but that was it. This called for a pit stop at Decathlon. *"Go on, you do the talking,"* said Dave, *"It's hilarious!"*

I boldly summoned a Decathlon assistant and announced, *"My good man, I wish to go sport climbing. Would you kindly furnish me with the required items?"*

The French teenager gave a very confused *"Quoi?"*

On arrival at Céüse, we pitched our tent at a farm in Sigoyer. This is as close to the crag as you can camp. It still leaves a good hour of walking every day. Something like camping in Llanberis and climbing on Cloggy. I was reading Peter Kay's book, The Sound of Laughter. Each night I would snigger myself off to sleep.

One night I woke abruptly at about 03:00 to rustling in the front porch. I drew breath and cursed. *"Dave, are you having a midnight feast?"* I enquired. *"Mate, that's not me!"*

Some beast of the night was trying to steal my saucisson! In a state of disoriented semi-slumber, I thought we were being invaded by a badger. I gave the instruction to Dave, *"Mate, they can be aggressive. Get tooled up."* Clutching a bottle of wine and a book, I quickly opened the front of the tent to reveal a panic-stricken fox who took one look at us and took flight.

I could imagine the cunning renard checking all the international vehicle plates on the campsite, believing he'd struck gold when he found a British number plate. He'd undoubtedly thought, *"Ah, les Anglais! Qu'est-ce qu'ils mangent beaucoup? Les poisons et les frites!"*

The climbing was world class, and made the hour-long plod every morning well worth the effort.

July 2005 The Alps

I guess I put my parents through quite a lot. In 2005 we had an amazing alpine season when we seemed to bounce from north face to north face. Climbing with one of my mates, the pace and momentum we achieved was brutal. On 2nd July we climbed the Dent Blanche above Ferpècle in Switzerland, descending from the mountain on the same day. Then we set off to climb the Walker Spur on the Grandes Jorasses on the 3rd July. The climb was straightforward and went according to plan.

Between the two climbs I made a call to the tourist information office giving them my plan and details. On completing the climb and descending the south face to Italy, I gave them another call to inform them we were down and now back in safety. We didn't hang around and jumped into Airforce 1, driving straight over to climb the Cassin route on the north face of Piz Badile. We'd stopped in a garage, and as usual, I was emptying the sandwich counter when my dad phoned my companion, asking if we were we ok. *"Fine thanks Bernie. As usual Pete's buying sandwiches. He really needs to do something about those worms."*

The PGHM (Peloton de Gendarmerie de Haute Montagne) had just called my parents to say we were missing on the Grandes Jorasses and a helicopter had been scrambled. Despite my phone call, the message that we were down and safe had somehow not been passed on.

April 2006 Chamonix, France

For seven long summers I had a simple routine. Risk life and limb on the north face of a particular mountain, party like it was the millennium. Then repeat. The contrast couldn't have been greater; beautiful Swiss chalets with manicured window boxes, brimming with alpine flowers but pan left and there's Pete from Wales in his old van. This all took place on the tightest of budgets. For two months every summer, I could be found in my van in Chamonix railway station car park. It was a way of life I enjoyed for seven years until I became a Mountain Guide. Then, and only then, could I afford to stay in mountain huts.

Over the Brink and Back

August 2006 France – Gaining Experience

Alpine climbing is a roller coaster of exceptional highs and lows. From blue skied, sun-drenched summits to freezing cold, storm bound nights. The complete alpinist takes it all in their stride, processes the learning points and moves on. The only important outcome is that everyone comes down from the mountain safely.

In fact, an alpinist without stories of epic retreats is either a boring drinking partner or, to put it bluntly, a liar.

In early August 2006 I had my first proper incident. As per usual, I was enjoying a long summer holiday in Chamonix. I had just upgraded Airforce 1 (my trusty old transit van) to a yellow and green ex-AA VW Transporter, dubbed the 'Brazilian'. Now having a full-time job, I was being flashy and treated myself to the luxury of a long-established campsite. I found myself on the famed 'sloping field' campsite in Argentière. It was a marked improvement on the station car park.

With the usual group of four friends, we made plans to head to the Tournier Spur on Les Droites. The day before the climb, excitement grew in the team as kit was packed and repacked. We put in a last-minute call to the Office de Haute Montagne to check conditions. The office stated *"pas bon"*. I only focused on *"bon"*! When it was revealed that conditions were actually poor, I joked that it was just sour grapes as London had got the 2012 Olympics, since Paris was the other major contender. I wouldn't have dreamt of taking clients on a difficult route in the forecast conditions but we were convinced that our team was strong enough to deal with them. So, we all assembled at the Grand Montets cable car.

The Argentière basin is a beautiful cirque. The skyline is as jagged as a saw blade, and quickly brought the attention of the group onto our objective, the one thousand metre pillar of granite that punctuated the skyline. Suddenly, the team very notably shifted into a higher gear. We snaked our way through the maze of crevasses and jumbled ice blocks that lie beneath the north face and set a very meaningful plod to the toe of the pillar. It was already 10:30. Leaving from the valley floor and approaching the route had taken longer than we had expected. We quickly geared up and prepared ourselves for two days of hard climbing.

The warmth of the mountain is a mixed blessing. Sensation returns to previously numb fingers and the body relaxes in the morning sun, whilst granite blocks the size of cars whistle down the north face as the nighttime freeze releases its frosty grip. Hearing quickly becomes your primary sense as you strain to listen to the thawing ice and for any incoming dangers above.

I took a wrong turn and climbed high onto the crest of the ridge. Thankfully, someone else had made the same error and had constructed a belay. I quickly used it and swung back onto the flank of the ridge to re-join the system of cracks that the climb followed. My team-mate was making good progress up the splitter granite cracks. We swung leads and quickly gained several hundred metres of height. The sun was starting to catch the vast north face.

A hundred metres below the brèche both our teams ground to a halt. The warm, friendly slabs that had given hours of pleasure as we gently but quickly padded upwards, now turned white with snow and ice. We pooled resources, had a brief chat and decided who should lead. (We drew straws for who should tell him.) By now it was early evening and long tiered shadows mottled the spur. We donned our crampons, clutched our axes and did battle with the final two pitches that signalled the end of the rock section. What had been lazy, enjoyable VS slab, quickly turned to exceptionally thin VII. Sparks quite literally flew, as crampons were carefully placed on match-thin edges and then flailed into the darkening skies. It was with great relief that we crawled onto the tiny granite ledges of the brèche.

Just behind us were two French Mountain Guides, enjoying a day off from their job at the Peloton de Gendarmerie de Haute Montagne (PGHM).

My partner, on our ledge, reluctantly shuffled just enough to allow me to park a bum cheek. Note the indefinite article – a bum cheek. Perched on a tiny ledge half a kilometre above the Argentière glacier, I flicked the burn button on my Jet Boil and watched as the flame melted several handfuls of snow for my pasta. Cheap and light-weight, pasta was a summer staple. I kept getting wafts of some delightful creation from the French quarters on the ledge below. As soon as the mind is allowed to wan-der, it feeds you a stream of false commentary. *"They've got brie and gallons of wine. Their ledge is palatial!"*

We'd been given good information about a piece of kit called a Blizzard Survival Bag. Essentially the Blizzard Bag is a tinfoil bivi bag. Light and compact, it sounded absolutely perfect. We'd all bought one for the climb and looked forward to a comfortable night's sleep. One of our team pointed out that should lightning occur the bag could also have similar properties to a Faraday cage.

By now it was dark and the temperature quickly dropped below freezing. I thought, I must try and get some rest before tomorrow. The exceptionally light-weight nature of the Blizzard Bag came from its minimal use of material. As I pulled it on, I realised the first design flaw. If you so much as moved an inch, the fabric rustled loudly. I pulled mine up and was amazed at how big it actually was. It just went on and on. I looked down and thought, *"That's odd I can see the glacier below my feet."* In the half-light, I'd torn the Blizzard Bag so now I just had a tinfoil tube!

The temperature dropped to around -5°C that night and sleep didn't come easily. I knew my ledge-mate was desperately cold too as every time he exhaled, he shuddered. Thinking it must soon be time to move I looked at my watch. It was only 23:30! Another 4 hours of pain to go. At 03:30 we made ready, boiled some coffee and ate a fruit bar. I stretched my wooden, numb legs, trying to encourage blood back to them.

I cursed at having to maintain balance on an icy ledge the size of a generous shelf. For all my cursing and bad morning temper, it was shaping up to be a beautiful day. The sky was becoming lighter, and the spur now struck out above us like the bow of a ship. I offered to tackle the first pitch. In all honesty I was just glad to get moving. I tied into the rope and got ready. I first had to teeter for 10 metres along a knife edge ridge. The ridge was flanked by 500m of precipitous nothingness. The ridge then abruptly met the vertical. I was all too aware I had 10 metres of horizontal rope out. To avoid crippling rope drag I must climb five vertical metres or so, before considering placing any kit to protect myself. This is the beauty of true alpinism. One minute you're sitting, shivering, stiff as a board. The next, you're climbing for your life.

Salvation and safety came in the form of a sling placed over a tiny flake. The sling kept lifting and required constant attention to ensure it remained seated. The climb now went from steep to vertical. I talked to myself to offer encouragement. *"Throw it, test it, pull on it."* The consequence of a fall from this point would have been unthinkable. The equipment was terrible, the sobering reality was that I'd pin ball down the granite spur and then disappear into a vertical abyss, either side of the narrow ridge. Just as I was contemplating the consequences, the quality of the snow-ice worsened. Continuing was out of the question. I glanced at the other four who were offering constant encouragement, and at the single, poor runner and then made the heart-breaking decision to throw the towel in. After several minutes of awkward down climbing I was in a position to gingerly weight the sling and return to the steep ridge. Now we were facing an epic descent. We knew we couldn't abseil yesterday's line as that followed the crest. If we followed the plumb line, we'd swing into a steep gully that was being racked by stone and ice fall.

"The route is in appalling condition and the descent is death. We've no other option but to call for a helicopter rescue. Good thing we are all insured." I said.

Disappointment struck the team. None of us had ever been in a situation where we couldn't get ourselves out of the trouble we had landed ourselves in before, and asking for help cuts deeply against the grain of any mountaineer. At the time it was a horrible decision to make. In time though, I've become far more comfortable with my plan. In any situation in the mountains, probability and consequence must be considered. In this case, the probabilities were that the sun would soon be touching the flanks of the spur and the daily torrent of cascading debris would start, and the consequences were that five people in a narrow couloir would be in a death trap, being bombarded by loose rock and ice and with their ropes and / or anchor compromised.

It was then that I demonstrated my proficiency in the French language. I phoned 112 to alert the authorities to the problem.

I quickly remembered that anything ending in 'tion' has a French origin. So, I said, *"Bonjour, extraction pour cinq alpinistes des Droits".*

A slightly stunned voice said, *"Hello, but where on the right are you?"*

"No, Les Droites le montagne, proche de Chamonix."

"Ah, I will call the PGHM."

At this point, team France made an appearance from stage left.

I explained that conditions were quickly deteriorating, and that we'd contacted the PGHM.

"But we are the PGHM!" they explain.

Hang on, I thought - this is quickly turning into a Monty Python sketch.

They produced a radio from their bag and, as we watched, a helicopter entered the cirque. It searched a spur a kilometre to the north on the Aiguille Verte. Our new French friends radioed the helicopter pilot to direct him to our location. There were now seven of us fighting for space. The approach for the helicopter was desperate. The col we were in consisted of a saddle formed by a narrow pillar of granite and the north face. After several attempts, it reversed in and quickly dropped a cable to our first climber. He gave us all a salute and was then quickly winched to safety. He was dropped off at the Argentière hut. Then, the next attempt was made. The helicopter was an Alouette III - a well proven, robust vehicle, but I have to admit it did then look a lot like a Citroen 2CV with blades.

It was now my turn. As the helicopter came into a stationary hover it produced a ton of down draft. I couldn't be simultaneously connected to the mountain and the helicopter, so I first dropped my mountain belay. This left me on a tiny ledge, unsecured, battling the down draft and violent noise overhead. It was with great relief that I attached the cable to my harness. The ascent was unreal. I was quite literally plucked off the mountainside and spinning like a top, winched quickly into the helicopter. As I arrived, the loadmaster pulled me into the rear seat. It was exactly like a 2CV. I was looking for the tape deck and ash tray. The helicopter landed on the roof of the Argentière hut. It was now that I made a monumental faux pas.

The Alouette is a small helicopter, so it has virtually no distance between the top of its door and its rotor blades. As the aircraft was flying straight off again it didn't shut down. I stand at 6'5" and was still wearing crampons. As I tried to stand bolt upright the loadmaster rugby tackled me and put me on the ground. Realising my mistake, I quickly apologised and then thanked him for his help. He shook his head, shut the door and was gone.

I caught my mate's eye, grinned and said, *"Well, that went well!"*

The other lads were all flown to the hut. The two PGHM Guides who were climbing behind us stayed in the aircraft and got a lift down to the valley. We started our long, silent plod down. That night we held court over several beers, pizzas, chips, garlic bread, crisps and gateau. We'd been into the mountains, had an epic adventure and safely returned. That's all that mattered. Within hours we drove through the Mt. Blanc tunnel and climbed the south ridge of the Aiguille Noir. Pride restored, once again we were on top of the world.

Over the Brink and Back

April 2009 Scotland – My Greatest Faux Pas

The British IFMGA Winter Test has a reputation for being brutally hard. Over five days you are put through a physical and mental test to examine your suitability to become a Mountain Guide and look after others in arctic conditions. Several friends of mine, whose opinion I respect, have described it as *"The Filter"*.

In 2010 my life was organised around accommodating one thing – the Guides' Scheme. That winter I juggled my work life, Guide assessment preparation and personal climbing. My diary was full.

The exam started with a two-day expedition. We were based at Glenmore Lodge near Aviemore, located in the heart of the Cairngorm National Park. It was an opportunity to demonstrate our competence in mountaineering, climbing and navigating whilst simultaneously looking after clients in Scottish winter conditions.

The day before, I packed and repacked my kit. I had condensed my equipment into a very 'European' sized rucksack, removing every extra gram of weight. I had even purchased a super lightweight snow shovel, made from carbon fibre.

The expedition set off at the crack of dawn. We were all keen to demonstrate our strength and fitness in the mountains. By 15:00 hours we had travelled a considerable distance, gained well over 1,000m in height and taken in a steep couloir.

The assessor stopped us and, in a broad Scottish accent, said, *"Right, dig me a snow profile and explain everything you see."* I quickly dropped my rucksack and pulled out my shovel handle then went for the blade. It wasn't there. It must be ... I checked again. No, it's definitely not there. In the frantic rush of packing and last-minute alterations I'd somehow left it behind. I'd be dragged over the coals for this.

The assessment team were now checking everyone's snow profile and listening to their observations. *"Pssssss pssssss!"* I got the attention of the next candidate and managed to borrow his shovel. A bullet dodged, we continued on our way.

We had now arrived at a bank of snow in a gully wall high on the Cairngorm plateau. We were asked to make a snow hole for the night and were reliably informed that somewhere there was already a hole dug in the bank. A few minutes probing and we located its position. I now had to excavate the remaining snow. But only had a shovel handle to do this with. As the assessment team were watching our every move, I shoved the handle into the snow to make it appear that it was connected to a blade and assumed more of a foreman's role, directing the other candidates, complimenting them on their progress and offering subtle changes to design, because we'd successfully located and enlarged an existing hole. The creation was monstrous. *"Can you see my light? Walk towards me!"* I, much relieved, joked with another candidate.

Over the Brink and Back

September 2010 Switzerland – Alpine Exam

I do not cheat, I merely stack the odds in my favour; a practice that gives me immense satisfaction!

During the alpine summer examination, we were told to meet in Kandersteg, Switzerland. Despite quizzing members of the assessment team, no clue was released as to where we were heading. I studied a map closely and shortlisted the nearby options. In total there were four possible mountain refuge destinations, all of which I would describe as esoteric. In the end I rang them and explained that my friend Mr. Ralphs was arranging bookings for a forthcoming trip. *"Has he made a reservation for 6 people on September the 4th?"* I drew blank several times. On my last roll of the dice, I called the Frunden Hutte. *"Yes, you are booked in for two nights."* Got you! With another candidate, I visited the hut a week before the exam. After a summer of guiding, your fitness and skills should be excellent but there's something so reassuring about knowing the terrain.

When I returned under exam conditions, the young couple running the hut both said, *"Hi Pete. How are you?"* I told the examining staff that I had met them ice climbing. The exam itself turned into quite a big day. We walked from the valley to the hut, a good 1,000 metres of ascent, and then continued onto the glacier to demonstrate our competence at crevasse rescue. After eight hours on the go and 1,000m of height gain I was ready to call it a day and head inside for food.

The hut guardian ran out and explained a party of three were stuck about 1,000m above us on a ridge known as the Gelletgrat. They had phoned the emergency services but because of the rapidly descending cloud base and the failing light the helicopter couldn't fly. We all exchanged glances, asked the hut guardian to fill our flasks and set off into a darkening sky.

I've long prided myself on my fitness. I was accompanied by a former Marine and a member of staff at the National Mountain Centre. We removed some layers of clothing, as we were going to be moving fast, and headed into the night. The guidebook reckoned the climb would take four to five hours, we did it in three.

In ascent, the ridge was straight forward, and we located the stricken Swiss team with no difficulties. Despite asking, they didn't have any brandy or Toblerone. Things became far more engaging on the descent. By now it was pitch black and the cloud base had descended making route finding a challenge. Added to that, it is imperative that the weaker party are physically below the Guides. In descent, this meant sending them first and issuing clear orders in German, *"Links, rechts, halt, papers!"* Despite being exhausted I still laughed at my own jokes. We arrived back at the hut at 02:30 after 20 hours on the go.

November 2010 – IFMGA Guide

My career begins aged 32.

There's something truly wonderful about leading others in the mountains. Aside from the breath-taking views you both get to enjoy; the hostile environment eats away every superficiality in a person's character until you can clearly see the raw person. Although during this time, both my client's and my eyes were constantly shaded by dark, glacier sunglasses, I believed I could often see deep into their soul. I forged many special friendships. Several ex-clients made the effort to come and see me during my two year 'mini-break' in hospital. I would often spend a week with a client 'bouncing' around the Alps, as we went from one mountain to another. At the end of that time, I'd drop a sunburnt, very tired, happy and always safe client off at the airport.

The mountain setting led to many admissions from clients: personal problems, worries and hilarious stories. I believe it is this time, and most especially this time alone with a client, that differentiates good Guides from great Guides. At the end of the week, I would always make a brief note about them, not just their physical abilities but also their lives. Twelve months later, though my memory about every client may not have been razor sharp, I could refer back and ask relevant questions, such as, *"So, how are sales of your book going?"*, that indicated that they were not just another client.

One of many amusing stories came from a client when we were climbing a route called the Hohlaubgrat on the Allalinhorn, Switzerland. The climb departs from a beautiful, Swiss mountain refuge called the Britannia Hut. Although the hut is readily accessible from the busy ski town of Saas Fee, it immediately immerses the climber in a wild landscape of snow, ice and rock.

I must warn you, this story is not for the faint hearted! My client had taken his colleagues for a night out in downtown London. They wound up in quite a famous night club. When the DJ arrived to play his set, his routine was that he would strut through a busy dance floor, flanked by bouncers. The crowd formed a corridor with the ladies each thrusting a hand forward. As the DJ passed, he would kiss their hands as he proceeded to his booth. A young member of my client's party said, *"Hey Boss watch this!"*. He put his hand down his pants and inserted his finger into his anus. Then as the DJ walked past, he stretched his arm out. His was duly kissed by the prima donna DJ as he strutted by. I almost fell off the climb in tears of laughter.

Spring 2011 Hardangervidda, Norway

It was a tranquil, spring day when the train to Finse drew out of Oslo station. Despite the optimism of an approaching summer, the implement with which the train was furnished told a different story. The front of the train was armed with a snowplough of medieval appearance and its massive engine nurtured a long line of sturdy carriages. The fact that, along with many of the passengers, I was boarding the train in full arctic attire, carrying my skis and wearing a large rucksack, indicated that this was no normal route. Finse, our destination, stands high on the Hardangervidda at 1,222 metres above sea level. The plateau would undoubtedly still be in deep, dark winter. Conversely, Oslo is a lofty 23 metres above sea level.

I had, only minutes ago, met my group of clients for the week ahead. Our plan was to retrace the journey taken by the Norwegian saboteurs in February 1943, as they attempted to beat the arctic conditions and Nazi patrols. Their goal was to destroy the stockpile of heavy water being amassed at the Vemork hydro-electric power station in Nazi-occupied Norway during World War II and thus prevent the Nazi development of atomic weapons. Their display of resilience and fortitude is, to me, unparalleled.

When the bell rang to forewarn us that the train was stopping, the immediate weather conditions in Finse became all too apparent. The hut that I'd visited several times before lay two hundred metres away in the cloud and driving snow. Before departing, I'd applied copious amounts of Blue Extra Wax to my Nordic skis. In an ambient temperature of -6°C and a wind speed of 40mph, I alighted from the train and stepped straight into my skis. The assault on one's senses when suddenly confronted by such conditions is unworldly. One minute I was talking to new clients in a centrally heated train carriage, the next I was wearing ski goggles, facing white out conditions and a powerful wind and spindrift. I gathered my team, and we followed the route markers to the hut.

The Norwegians have an excellent infrastructure of mountain huts. A centrally run organisation known as the Norwegian Trekking Association (DNT) own, maintain and provision a huge network of mountain refuges across Norway. After a wild 200 metre walk, we arrived at Finse DNT hut. It is much bigger than the other huts and is permanently manned.

I introduced myself and my group to the staff and then loaded tomorrow's route coordinates into my GPS device. I have a system that works perfectly for me. I write every Easting and Northing onto my map, then highlight the numbers with red and green highlighter pen. GPS way marker points are written on and highlighted in blue. This system offers clarity and ease of use when fighting Arctic winds and driving snow. My thoughts are with the heavy water saboteurs of 1942. Absolutely everything is on my side; I'm skiing between well provisioned huts, en route, my Garmin GPS updates my location every few minutes and despite seemingly being in the wilderness, I constantly maintain three bars of coverage on my phone. The saboteurs had only a basic, military issue sighting compass; they were weighed down with heavy weapons, ammunition and explosives for the raid, and, in pursuit, was a fiercely determined and lethal foe.

By mid-March the weather on the Hardangervidda becomes very volatile. Our crossing was no exception. By night the temperature dropped to -18°C, by day it hovered around -6°C. Squally fronts constantly battered the team, reminding us how serious the location can be. Only days before our departure, three Britons had perished whilst attempting the traverse.

The route crosses many frozen lakes. I unclip my rucksack waist strap in readiness to jettison its weight should the worst happen. By night, the huts come alive with noise, chatter and laughter. By day, your head is buried deeply in the back of your hood as you attempt to block out the driving snow and howling wind.

After five long days the crossing was finally over and we reached Rjukan. A gentle and relaxed ski into the village saw our arrival at a warm, welcoming hostel and we celebrated with a bottle of red. On arrival in Rjukan the saboteurs then had to conduct the raid and escape into neutral Sweden!

Over the Brink and Back

Winter 2011 - 2012 Scotland

After guiding in the Himalaya in the autumn (an attempt on Trisul), it was back to Scotland for the winter. One organisation I worked for owned a property in the Kyle of Lochalsh. It led to some quite simply amazing experiences. With two keen, fit students and a Land Rover, I'd drive to the Northwest Highlands of Scotland for a week of winter mountaineering. On arrival at the gothic looking manor house, I'd simply call a number and, very like the Adams family, a cook and housekeeper would appear. The terrain, that could easily be accessed from the property, was just staggeringly good. Torridon and Skye lay a stone's throw away. I was like a child in a sweet shop, and judging by the size of the pantry a very well provisioned sweetshop at that.

In the cirque at the back of Beinn Eighe lies the remote, precipitous and neck-achingly impressive Triple Buttress. We opted for the easy but impressive Fuselage Gully. Its name derives from the fuselage of an Avro Lancaster that still sits chocked in its narrows, its propeller forming a running belay. Tragically, the aircraft was lost with all crew members when it clipped the summit, sending it catapulting onto the mountain's flanks.

Climbing on the northerly aspect of these mountains really gives a comprehension of location, a true sense of wilderness. We were afforded mind-blowing views north towards Ullapool and the Hebrides. In 40mph winds we made the summit before battling an incessant head wind as we descended into the glen.

During that week, I learned a very important lesson in mountaineering. On descending in poor weather from the summit of Beinn Alligin, another Torridonian giant, I drifted a few degrees off course and hit a neighbouring spur. After five minutes of futile descent, I realised the error, admitted my mistake, and started the heart-breaking plod back uphill. You'll only do that once! When descending from a summit, imagine you're following the spokes of a wheel. A small error initially, is quickly amplified to a real problem. The lesson? Always take a quick bearing as you leave the summit, no matter how confident you are. It's a horrible moment when you admit your fault and witness the expressions of disappointment and fatigue on your students' faces.

After a great week of adventure, I returned the Land Rover and students and headed home to the mountains, cliffs and waves of Wales.

March 2013 Austria – Easter Holiday

Several weeks before my accident I had a leisurely Easter break, ski touring with a friend, Guy Buckingham. We decided to try a multi-day journey in the Tyrol region of Austria.

We left the van in Obergurgl and caught the Hohe Mut cable car. It quickly carried us deep into the Tyrol range. The weather was cloudy but bright and stable, allowing for moderate visibility. I stepped into my skis and cautiously began picking my way down the steep west face that defines the start of the tour.

Out of the corner of my eye, I spotted movement then heard a blood curdling scream. A fellow ski tourer had fallen the length of a narrow chute and lay motionless at its base. My companion and I skied the 50 metres over to where he lay. His distorted body had come to a halt in a steep, avalanche chute, in a far from an ideal location.

Guy quickly cut and insulated a ledge in the snow, whilst I climbed down to the casualty to make a primary survey of his injuries. The other members of his group arrived and were obviously panicked by the situation. This is where my voluntary mountain rescue experience really came into its own. I had attended numerous accidents, each unique, presenting a different challenge and requiring a different solution. You quickly grow accustomed to the sight of blood and distorted limbs and appreciate the requirement for pace.

The skier was conscious but in a great deal of pain. On impact he had shattered his femur. I now had to quickly decide whether we should attempt to move him out of the avalanche chute or have him airlifted from his current spot. The cloud was light and the temperature steadily building. I was gravely concerned about our location but recognised any movement would be agonisingly painful for him and that the potentially jagged nature of the break could damage his femoral artery, which indicated very careful movement was required. On the other hand, although the avalanche risk forecast was category 2, it was sunnier than forecast and there was a large catchment area above, making the gulley a dangerous place to linger. Speed would be of the essence. Guy and I manhandled him as carefully as possible out of the chute and onto the prepared ledge. I called for a helicopter, giving our grid reference and altitude, and within minutes one arrived.

The winchman was lowered down to us. He saw my IFMGA badge and introduced himself as a fellow Mountain Guide. The casualty was secured into a strop and quickly winched to safety.

I suspect I met that winchman again, soon after.

Rock climbing – Arapiles, Australia

cliff climbing Llithfaen, North Wales

Climbing at the depot, Manchester

Skiing on my day off a week before the accident, Austria

The Chardonnet Couloir, Haute Route

the Tournier Spur, Les Droites

turn

A spectacular ride to safety

Deposited on the roof of the Argentière hut

Teaching snow science

My van, the Brazilian – Saas Grund

A typical day at work – the summit ridge of Weissmies

A huge avalanche in the Tyrol – Scotty's tracks are just above where the slab failed

Last of the daylight on the Brittle Ledges – Eiger, 1938 route

A brutal white out – The Hardangervidda, Norway

The Hinterstoisser Traverse – Eiger, 1938 route

climbing in Rjukan, Norway

The first bivouac on the Peuterey Integral

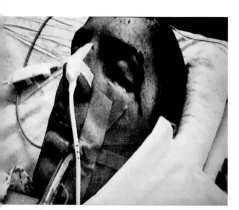

April 2013, in intensive care

Nine years later, cycling through Switzerland

Nine years after the accident, cycling in the Écrins, France

April 2013 Austria – The Aftermath

At the foot of the cliff, the avalanche debris pushed my unconscious body into a river.

That should have been it ... I should have drowned. For once though, fate stepped in and was on my side. Somehow my rucksack floated (I assume due to air inside it) and it supported my unconscious head, making rescue possible.

I fell exactly 140 metres (460 feet), like falling from the Blackpool Tower. As I was located in a deep ravine, the helicopter tried using its full reserve of cable but still came up short. They then employed a technique called long-lining. The winchman used a reserve rope and attached that to the cable, resulting in a very long length of cable and rope. The winchman was then gingerly lowered into the gorge to retrieve a seemingly lifeless me. The technique had worked.

I was helicoptered to Innsbruck hospital. On arrival, my core temperature had fallen to 28°C. I was severely hypothermic. Forty-two minutes after the accident I was undergoing brain surgery, having shards of skull removed from my brain.

Initial tests on my brain sought to establish the extent of the damage. It was quantified by using the Glasgow Coma Scale (GCS), a scale that scores an individual from 3-15. My initial score was 3 – even a stone could manage this! Another vital figure was my intra-cranial pressure. As a result of the injuries incurred and the surgery, my brain quite literally swelled. If the pressure had surpassed 140mmHg, I would have required further surgery to remove a section of skull. My intra-cranial pressure hovered at 140mmHg for several days and I was prepared to be rushed back into theatre. As a result of this pressure my temperature regulation went mad. I required a very specialist machine that effectively pumped my circulating blood through a 'fridge' in a desperate attempt to lower my core temperature. All of this required 1:1 nursing with a constant watch being kept on me and my medical equipment. The electrical activity of my brain was also assessed and found to be minimal.

I was totally unaware that any of this was happening. As far as I was concerned, I could have been enjoying an extended lie-in at Hotel Innsbruck!

Anna:

After the accident Pete was on the Intensive Care Unit at Innsbruck Hospital. We knew that his accident had been extremely severe, that he had sustained multiple injuries, including substantial brain injuries but we had no sense of what that would mean for Pete's future or for ours. My overriding memory of the early days is of the distress of the accident but also how stressful I found it leaving home to go to Austria. It seems ridiculous now that I even worried about it, but my son was only six months old. I had never been away from him and I found it incredibly stressful leaving him, particularly in such distressing circumstances.

In the early days we spent as much time as possible at Pete's bedside; visiting times were restricted and only two visitors were allowed in at a time. We took it in turns and spent hours talking to him. He was in a terrible way, the impact of the trauma clearly visible on every part of his body. He required extensive medical input to keep him alive and those first few weeks were full of extreme highs and lows, of hope and gravest fear. Pete had a deep wound above his left eye (the least of his worries in comparison to his other injuries). I remember watching the skin heal as the days ticked by, marvelling at what his body was doing and taking it as a good sign that, despite the magnitude of his injuries, he was healing.

Pete had been a larger-than-life character and at six feet five inches tall, he had a real physical presence about him. He had travelled extensively and had had more adventures than most people would have in a lifetime. He told many tales of near misses and close encounters; he'd always come out on top though and Dad often referred to him affectionately as 'Golden Balls'. We all held a deep hope, hope-against-hope, that this would turn into another one of those tales and that, against all the odds, Pete would come out unscathed with another great story for the pub. Mum and Dad stayed in Innsbruck for the duration, as did Pete's then partner. My two sisters and I went to and fro as and when we were able. My brother-in-law, Gareth, who is a medical professional, visited in the early days too, his presence was very comforting to Mum and Dad, but he was only able to reinforce the gravity of the situation. My sister, Kate, went out in the first few days and then I arrived as she left. I was in Innsbruck when Jane arrived; we had all awaited her assessment of the situation. It was some time since Gareth had left and Pete's condition was unstable and changing daily. Jane has significant experience of ICU (Intensive Care Unit) care and we all eagerly awaited her opinion, again holding on to the hope that she might be able to offer some reassurance or glimmer of light. She couldn't; the situation was desperate and while we clung onto phrases like "He's in the best possible place and getting the best care" they offered little comfort.

I remember further profound disappointment when Pete's sedation was reduced and then further reduced, and nothing happened. Reality was setting in slowly; this wasn't ever going to become just another tale for the pub. The accident was going to be life-changing for Pete; this was just the very beginning, and the future was uncertain and terrifying.

Val:

It was the grimmest of times. Bernie and I were plucked from home in the early hours of the morning as was Pete's former partner. We were all too stunned and anxious to talk on the journey; it felt as though this was not actually happening, not Pete, not a horrific accident ... total disbelief. We knew little of the detail of the situation and eventually arrived at Innsbruck Hospital and sat in the bleak ICU waiting room, waiting for a doctor to meet us. Her response to our query as to the seriousness of Pete's accident was provided in broken English, "Peter may die". Numbed, we were allowed to see Pete two at a time. It was devastating. Our incredibly fit, fun-loving, and lively son was on full life support in an induced coma surrounded by machines, display screens and drips. No words can describe how we felt.

The next few days got worse. Visiting hours were strictly limited to two sessions per day with only two visitors at a time. At every visit there seemed to be more bad news, more machines and more equipment to keep Pete alive. We were told to stay near the hospital so that we could come quickly if he deteriorated further. Bernie and I remember waking each morning, relieved that Pete had made it through the night but then the anxiety would return, building up through the morning until afternoon visiting time. We felt in a total daze, trapped in the beautiful city of Innsbruck, surrounded by tourists enjoying the lovely spring. Visits from Kate, Jane, Anna and Gareth were a huge comfort, but we were also very worried about the impact of the accident on them and their families. It really was the grimmest of times; a seemingly never-ending terrible dream and desperate desire to get back to life as it was. I will leave it to Pete to continue.

Over the Brink and Back

May 2013 Birmingham –
Return to the UK

I remained on the edge of life for weeks. Still in a coma and still on life support, I eventually stabilised sufficiently to be flown back to the UK. One of my enduring disappointments is that I missed all this excitement! Just imagine having your own plane and your own medical team. No check in. No habitual trips to Costa. No chance to stroll past all the allegedly 'Duty Free' yet very expensive merchandise. I can only hope that the medical team gave me the full safety briefing:

"Exits are located ... here, here and here. If we land (Land? Is this a joke?) *on water, your life jacket will be useless as the seawater is about 6°C and the water pressure will probably stop you opening the exits anyway ... "*

I was flown back home to the UK on a ventilator. Apparently, my private jet was welcomed by an ambulance and eight police motorcyclists whose job it was to surround the ambulance whilst I was in transit (or was it a Berlingo?). In the Queen Elizabeth Hospital, Birmingham, I was fitted with a tracheostomy. I like to think that this was to 'shut me up' should I awaken. In fact, it was to protect my lungs from silent aspiration and pneumonia. Apparently, I did go on to develop pneumonia whilst still floating around somewhere out there. Relying solely on knowledge gained during my HSE First Aid in the Workplace qualification, I'll bet it was only a raspy cough!

Anna:

Sometime after the accident, Pete was deemed stable enough to be transferred back to the UK. The trip was planned and then cancelled when Pete deteriorated. My understanding is that Pete was flown to Birmingham in a scaled-down ICU in the back of a huge plane. We were desperate to have him closer to home, but it felt like a gamble since his condition was still fluctuating and he still required intensive support just to keep him alive. The transfer was successful, and Pete arrived in Birmingham in May 2013. The transfer took its toll though and Pete's condition deteriorated again.

I think by this time he was no longer sedated and that an unsuccessful attempt was made to extubate him. Pete then had to have a tracheostomy and a PEG (percutaneous endoscopic gastrostomy) tube for direct feeding into his stomach. He remained dangerously ill. I remember visiting him on ICU in Birmingham and his eyes were looking in different directions, something he now finds hilarious!

I also remember the bleakest of conversations with a Neuro ICU consultant. Mum, Dad and I were taken to a family room where the impact of Pete's injuries was explained to us. The doctor spent time explaining the impact of the focal head injury (his head hit rock, requiring surgery to remove fragments of skull bone from his brain) but emphasised that the major concern was the diffuse axonal injury from falling / cartwheeling 140 metres. This was explained to us as being like 'shaken baby syndrome'; injury to every part of the brain, truly diffuse. No-one could predict what this would mean for Pete and his future, but it was as bleak and as grave as it could possibly be. The phrase that stays with me was something along the lines of "Pete's condition is likely to remain close to vegetative, but he may, in time, be able to communicate through blinking". I don't have a full memory of the meeting, but I do remember Mum and Dad's distress and that I couldn't stop my teeth from chattering.

Val:

We had longed for Pete to be transferred back to the UK but dreaded this move as he was still so extremely ill. We had to fly back approximately eight hours ahead of him. It was incredibly difficult leaving Pete behind in Innsbruck, knowing the risk of his journey. We were at the Queen Elizabeth Hospital when he eventually arrived and was transported past us into ICU. Pete looked dreadful. He was lying on his side on the stretcher, unconscious and completely grey. Yet again we feared he wouldn't survive the night. We were bundled into a tiny room and again bluntly told the extent of his injuries and that he might not survive. Hence began three more weeks of twice daily visits, procedures and more consultations.

I spent three weeks in intensive care in the Queen Elizabeth Hospital, being nursed much of the time on a one-to-one basis (there had to be some perks to this situation) before being transferred to ICU at Salford Royal Hospital, Manchester, nearer to my parents' home.

June 2013 Manchester – Another Transfer

Anna:

At the end of May, Pete was transferred to ICU at Salford Royal Hospital, then to HDU (High Dependency Unit) and then he was moved to a ward. This progress should have been cause for celebration. Pete was now out of danger. We knew he was going to live but the horrific impact of the situation was becoming apparent. I remember visiting Pete when he was still on a medical ward, awaiting transfer to a more specialist Neuro Rehab ward. It was clearly not the right place for him. The day was boiling hot; Pete was in a normal, hospital bed, lying unable to move, in full sunlight. He was extremely distressed, his left side moving restlessly and incessantly. I also remember feeling conflicted about Pete's friends visiting; I hated them seeing him like this. I felt sure the 'old Pete' would not have wanted anyone to see him so compromised.

I have no recollection of ICU, HDU or the general medical ward at Salford Royal. My awareness only started to return when I reached the Neuro Rehab ward.

Gradually waking up in Salford was hardly compatible with my amazingly clear and lucid memories of living and working in the Alps. To compound this, I slowly realized that I was unable to move – or to speak, at all. During 25 years of climbing and mountaineering and many years of work in the great outdoors, I can legitimately claim to have made the acquaintance of some unbelievably robust individuals. Epic ascents, near death climbing epics, scary near misses and massive post-climb celebrations were all part of my existence. However, nothing, absolutely nothing could prepare me for the distress I experienced as the coma-inducing drugs wore off. Whist trapped in this world, my life was one of perpetual fear and panic. I couldn't turn it off, it just went on and on and on.

It is perhaps best explained by using the example of the scene in the film Train Spotting, where the character Mark Renton, a heroin addict, goes 'cold turkey' and finds himself locked in a tiny bedroom … climbing the walls. It is as close to hell as the mind can imagine.

The doctor told my family, *"It is possible that Pete can hear. Try putting some headphones on him."* I was duly played Ben Howard, non-stop. I hate Ben Howard! That probably woke me prematurely.

Although the torment was sheer hell, I could only experience it because my body and brain were still just about functioning. There was one wonderful thing about such agony; it was far preferable to being dead!

I've stood on the summits of mountains in crisp morning light, climbed in the Himalaya and Alps, skied deep, fresh, powder snow, feared for my life on bold run-out climbs, felt the power of a hollow wave and visited the darkest pit of the human mind. I have done all that and somehow made it back alive and in one piece.

Val:

It was so good to have Pete in Salford Royal. Bernie and I were able to move home and travel to the twice daily visiting sessions. After ICU, HDU and the medical ward, we were pleased when Pete was moved to the Neuro Rehab ward. I have two special memories in the early days on this ward when Pete's tracheostomy was fitted with a speaking valve. Day after day we tried to get him to speak, to no avail. One afternoon Bernie and I were visiting Pete and Bernie went to get an extra chair. I said "Hello Pete, oh I wish you would speak." From behind the valve came a croaky "Mum". That was the first word Pete had spoken since the accident, the first word that indicated he understood what was being said. Bernie returned with the chair to find me in tears but for a change, these were tears of joy! We had to wait a few days for the next word, "Dad" this time.

Shortly after that, we held up a piece of paper with three names in large letters: Pete, Ian, Dave. We asked Pete if he could point to his name. Slowly his left hand came up and stabbed at "Pete"; more tears! For many

days we progressed this with a selection of house num-
bers, places, sisters' names, cars etc. Pete got them all
right. What a relief after a prognosis of a vegetative state.

The human brain in crisis is an incredibly tormented
organ. At first my memory was completely shot. I could
not start a conversation because:

I couldn't speak.

I forgot any point I was about to make.

I knew that if this persisted, I was in real trouble. Initially, I couldn't remember my age. I was 35 although,
with total sincerity, I maintained I was 21. Why 21?
I had no idea. An occupational therapist came to see
me asking me some unbelievably easy questions: *"Pete,*
what's 10 plus 3?" I could handle addition and sketched
13 on my talking board. She then asked: *"What's 5 mi-*
nus1?" The whole concept of subtraction was alien to
me. It's not as though I had a rough stab at it and said
"2". It totally baffled me. I needed someone to say: *"I*
have five cups of coffee and take one away. How many
remain?" The answer would have been obvious – Not
nearly enough!

To promote my memory, my hospital wall was covered
with photos. I can still remember them, family photos, a
photograph of Careless Torque (a short, hard climb on
the Plantation Boulders at Stanage Edge in Derbyshire)
and a picture of a glass of Rioja, my favourite wine.

After some weeks, I remember my internal dialogue
returning. I distinctly recall hearing a voice in my head.

My sister, Jane, visited me in hospital. *"Do you ever hear voices in your head?"* I asked her. Poor girl must have thought I was totally mad! For me it was that slow but sure return of internal discourse, that voice in my head, which marked a huge turning point, a full speed ahead acceleration of my rehabilitation. When Richard Hammond crashed the Vampire dragster during a shoot for Top Gear, incurring serious head injuries, he experienced the same phenomenon as his recovery kicked in. My brain was trying to heal! In my teenage years, I'd had a personal tutor. Once again, she visited me, setting me basic maths questions ... SOHCAHTOA (Some Officers Have Curly Auburn Hair Till Old Age) was still in there; it just needed dusting off.

Shortly after 'waking up', I received a phone message from Yvonne Chouinard. A friend who works for the outdoor equipment company, Patagonia, and had asked Chouinard (a renowned and respected US climber and businessman) to call me. He said *"Pete, don't worry, I was caught in a huge avalanche, it took about three years to fully recover from it. Stick with it, you'll be fine."* Weird ... I was lying, barely conscious, in a hospital ward, receiving a phone call from Yvonne Chouinard!

The human brain is a good bit of kit. On reflection, that is a grotesquely inappropriate understatement ... It is amazing!

Of the two weeks prior to my accident and for months afterwards I am unable to remember a single thing. Prior to that date, my memory is surprisingly lucid.

Distant memories return

* * *

The hypnotic rumbling of the surf rocked me gently off to sleep. I awoke six hours later to what sounded like exploding sticks of dynamite resonating around the beach.

"Yes, it's here!"

We had been tracking a deep low-pressure system that was sitting in Fitzroy and Sole. It would unquestionably send us 'gang-buster' surf. We were parked up in the Basque town Zarautz, due east of Saint Sebastián. I peered out of the window in the half light of morning and my suspicions were confirmed: the lazy four-foot swells of the previous day had been replaced with solid ten-foot corduroy.

I wasn't sure which emotion to go with … excitement or fear? Until that day I had climbed and surfed all over the world but nothing, absolutely nothing, breeds fear like a big, wild sea.

The line-up, or take off point, appeared to move before my eyes. When we went to bed it was 150 metres out. Now we had to negotiate 500 metres of heart-stopping impact zone before we were even remotely near a spot where we could catch a wave …

* * *

I woke up to one of my companions, Stu MacDonald, putting his crampons back on. The Brittle Ledges had offered us sanctuary for the night. A place to rest and regroup but that was all. The time was 04:00 and the three of us gazed ahead at the Traverse of the Gods. To this point the fierceness of the North Wall of the Eiger had not relented one bit. With Stu on the sharp end, we embarked on what is unquestionably the most exposed pitch of climbing I have ever experienced. Two kilometres below our heels the tiny village of Kleine Scheidegg was waking up to a stellar alpine day. As we brachiated across the Traverse of the Gods the deities appeared to smile on us ... soon we were standing on the infamous White Spider. Reaching this 60° ice smear, we tiptoed upwards on the front points of our crampons, just a couple of millimetres of steel biting in, heading to the seriously gearless exit chimneys ... A long way to go yet, but I felt I could almost touch the sun!

* * *

We shared nervous glances as we secured our leashes before paddling out into the mountainous swell. We knew this day would give us life-enduring memories.

I stand at 1.98 metres. That means that as I pop up for a wave, I will be staring down almost 4 metres into the trough! I waited for a lull between the sets then dashed out into the water. I was only too aware that the lull would be a short-lived, temporary affair, providing a few minutes respite before another set of enormous, powerful waves bore down upon us. This thought focused my mind and hurried my paddling ...

* * *

After three days of difficult and perilous mountaineering we finally reached the summit of the eminent Eiger. This was a climb of massive importance to me. At the age of 27, I had finally completed the prerequisite selection of alpine routes to be accepted into training to become a member of the IFMGA. Success on this climb was the result of huge effort and a 20-year obsession.

* * *

My last clear memory, pre-accident, is enjoying Easter with one of my friends, skiing up the Gran Paradiso, and savouring Italian cappuccino and dinner in Chamonix. I think my mind has said to my memory *"You won't like the next instalment. Let's hit delete all. This file is definitely corrupt!"*

Thus, for those months my mind is totally blank.

Anna:

Pete's first few weeks on the Neuro Rehab ward were spent having lots of therapy sessions, as he gradually regained awareness. He was popular amongst the nursing and therapy staff – it's probably not run of the mill having a young, motivated patient. He was eventually able to speak, albeit with a very slurred speech that was difficult to understand. He was substantially compromised cognitively and for many weeks suffered post-traumatic amnesia, but his long-term memory was crystal clear. This made visiting much easier; it gave conversations a focus and meant that Pete could meaningfully engage with his friends and reminisce. All of this, the speaking, the reminiscing, the human contact, was therapy for Pete. Ever since the accident, Pete's friends have played an important part in his rehab.

Over the Brink and Back

Manchester – Rehab Continues

Whilst in my twenties, working in a school in North Wales, both pupils and teaching staff attended school assembly every Friday. This assembly consisted of general notices and an inspirational reading from either the headmaster or the school chaplain. One Friday, after notices were given, the headmaster stared out at the crowd of three hundred people and, in quite an aggressive tone, shouted:

*"NEVER GIVE UP! DON'T YOU DARE
EVER GIVE UP!"*

Eight years later, I found myself lying in a hospital bed, totally unable to move my right side, staring at a hospital ward ceiling. I lay there for weeks, adrift with my thoughts. I stumbled upon the words of that headmaster and thought, right, Pete, it really is now or never.

Completely unable to stand, I was hoisted into a fully supportive wheelchair. This was dreadfully confusing. I didn't understand what was happening and hated the hoist. *"Never give up. Don't you dare ever give up!"*

To begin with, my efforts were like those of Uma Thurman in the film Kill Bill … I literally had to will my right leg to function at all. I found that if I focused all my attention and efforts, I could make tiny movements with my toes. After a day or so of sporadic movements my right foot touched the end of the bed. This gave me such hope; an initial and definitive sign of progress. The ball is rolling. This will be a challenge like no climb or mountain, but when is a great climb easy? Never.

Touching the end of my bed led to pressing the end of my bed. I can't begin to describe the joy and pleasure this simple act gave me. I thought I'd never move again, yet here I was actually pressing the end of my bed with my toes! I pressed the end of my bed for days, awakening the muscle fibres that had laid dormant for months. I became aware of the sensation returning to my right-hand side, the dark side of the moon.

My mental approach to rehabilitation was simple; create two boxes in my mind. Name one of them 'Problem' and the other 'Inconvenience'. As thoughts ran through my head, I threw them into the appropriate box.

Now, first and foremost, *"Has anyone else been injured?"* I ask my dad. He replies quickly *"No, Pete. You shouted a warning. As a result, you were the last man and the avalanche only caught you."* Now that news made me smile. A massive weight had just been lifted off me. I had done what a Guide would be expected to do and ensured the safety of my clients. No longer a problem. OK, down to business.

I can't stand, let alone walk. That can definitely go in the 'Problem' box.

I have a deep-seated love of Techno and Drum and Base music. My sister brought my favourite piece, Music by LTJ Bukem ... the soundtrack to my life. Its uplifting beat envelops me, and with my one functioning hand I grab the side of the bed and jiggle my right leg (the problem) into the void of fresh air. I do this for days, encouraged by the physios, slowly growing in strength and confidence. Eventually, after many weeks, with physio support and although listing to port, I am standing!

I love physio sessions ... the feeling that I am proactively taking control of the situation. Once again, I am the boss. I am no longer a passenger in life. I can set my own course and trim the sails. I was lucky enough to have a wonderful physio called Sal. Sal started the rehabilitation ball rolling.

It was with my physio and her colleagues that I eventually took my first tentative steps, months after the accident. A group of physios and nurses stood around me, ready to catch me if I were to fall. I grinned inwardly and thought, I'm 14 stone and six feet five inches and as a result of numerous falls off climbs, being 'fielded' by incredibly strong, athletic friends, I know that, if I fall, you don't have a chance of stopping me. I wore a plastic band sporting my hospital ID number and the words, 'Rowlands: severe risk of falling'. No, I thought, severe risk of being caught in an avalanche!

Years ago, I tried the famous Ron Fawcett route Supersonic, a bold E5 6a on High Tor, situated above Matlock Bath, Derbyshire. Reaching for the finishing holds, fatigue overtook me, and I arced through the sky, falling fifty feet. I wondered what my belayer would say if he saw my ID band ... something like *"What have you told the hospital about Supersonic?"* I sent him a photo of the ID band.

My first walk down the length of the hospital corridor was the single most important achievement of my life thus far. I was utterly terrified at the prospect and could only think of numerous reasons not to leave my bed. I ran a quick mental risk assessment:

I'm wearing a protective helmet. If I collapse and hit my head, I'm protected. Physios are here to help me.

Then, as I was in the habit of asking myself each time I started up a climb:

"What could possibly go wrong?"

Two physios supported me as I limped and swayed a full fifteen metres, the length of the corridor. OMG! I thought I'd never move again, and I've actually just walked 15 metres!

September 2013 –
Distressing News

Rehab was progressing well, but then my situation took a totally unexpected turn for the worse.

The doctor thought I might have damaged the arteries in my neck when my rucksack pulled tight in the fall, so I was sent for an ultrasound scan. I was diagnosed with stage 2A Hodgkin's Lymphoma, an aggressive cancer of the lymph glands. Now, when people say, *"You were so unfortunate to be caught in an avalanche"*, I have to disagree. The avalanche probably saved my life – without this early diagnosis, I could have been dead in approximately 18 months! The other positive aspect to this twist of fate is that due to the horrendous nature of the head injury I had sustained, I promptly forgot the diagnosis and only remembered I had cancer when chemotherapy commenced!

Val:

Pete was referred for investigations as he had had a small cluster of seizures, common whilst recovering from brain injury. The investigations included an ultrasound scan of his neck to see if a carotid artery had been damaged in the accident. I went with Pete and watched as the sonographers did the scan. It soon became obvious that something was wrong. The atmosphere changed from 'jokey' to serious and the probe was repeatedly moved to one area and measurements taken. Pete asked what was happening and was told there appeared to be an enlarged lymph gland. He asked if it could be cancer and was told that the gland would need to be removed and sent for tests; it could be many things although cancer could not be ruled out. Pete took this totally in his stride, saying "Lightning never strikes twice". Yet again, I was filled with dread.

Two weeks later, I sat stunned and silent with a doctor and nurse as they told me the diagnosis: Hodgkin's Lymphoma. I remember screaming silently in my head that this was just too much for Pete and for all the family. Five months after the accident and just as Pete was making progress with his rehab, to have this diagnosis was so very cruel. That evening Anna and Bernie visited Pete whilst I sat in the canteen with Pete's then partner.

Anna:

We were all aghast and devastated to get an incidental diagnosis of Hodgkin's Lymphoma, cancer of the lymphatic system. An unbelievable and cruel blow; Pete was already so incredibly vulnerable and facing an uncertain future. The family was already exhausted from months of anxiety and distress. This latest development was difficult to comprehend.

108

Dad and I sat on the edge of Pete's hospital bed and told him the results of the tests. He was distraught. I remember feeling exhausted afterwards and so worried about how Mum and Dad would find the physical and emotional reserves to deal with this ridiculously cruel blow. More uncontrollable teeth chattering on the drive back to Sheffield.

Andy:

We visited Pete in hospital. Ian was over from Australia. It was a harrowing experience, but Pete was amazingly positive and displayed a terrific recall of past epics and misdemeanours! Ann and I continued to visit Pete.

Chemotherapy: how bad can it really be? I mean, I was an International Mountain Guide. I've climbed the North Face of the Eiger. I expect I'll have it all done and be 'home' for a late lunch.

However, I had an abrupt reality check when my body reacted badly after the first dose. I was aware of an increase in movement around me. Doctors and nurses appeared rapidly from nowhere and began administering other medication and scrutinising my temperature as it rocketed. All I could think about was how uncomfortable the situation had become. I couldn't stop my teeth chattering. The sensation was exactly like I experienced sometimes when surfing. When you get out of the water on a cold, windy day, the wind cuts through your wetsuit like a knife through butter, stealing every single calorie of warmth. Bizarre really, people were desperately trying to save my life whilst I lay there thinking about the discomforts of surfing. Eventually the situation was brought under control, and I was loaded onto a trolley, complete with my own oxygen cylinder. The Chemotherapy Department phoned ahead and warned the ward staff that I had gone into shock but was now stable. On arrival back at the ward, two nurses ran over and enquired how I was. I managed to say, *"It might have killed a lesser man!"*

Anna:

Pete endured three months of chemotherapy while still in Salford Royal. This had the temporary effect of seriously limiting his rehab potential. He was exhausted and had numerous medical teams visiting, not to mention lengthy chemo trips to another department in the hospital. During this time Pete was in a wheelchair; I remember the horror of seeing his first proper wheelchair. It was a full-on machine complete with head support. I was upset at how disabled he looked in it.

Pete had been told that, as a side-effect of the chemotherapy, he would lose his hair. After a few treatment sessions he was proud to still have a full head of hair. On completion of his treatment, it had thinned ever so slightly but he still had a full head of hair. We all have somewhat wayward hair and we laughed about the fact that it would take more than a course of chemo to destroy our mops. I remember Pete joking that NASA were on their way to collect samples, to use in their new spacesuits.

110

The rounds of chemotherapy took their toll. Through the precise use of a toxic concoction of drugs, the doctor tries to kill the cancer cells without killing you. Unfortunately, the drugs also destroy your body's immune system (white blood cells) and lower your platelet count (cells involved in blood clotting).

It's a very simple test of which will 'blink' first; your body or the cancer.

I was moved from my four-bedded ward into a sterile side room and only allowed one visitor per day, my mum, who had to wear a surgical mask, apron, etc. I was repeatedly loaded onto a trolley and pushed to the Chemotherapy Department for my treatments. Their effect is cumulative.

After three months, luckily, the cancer blinked first!

Over the Brink and Back

January 2014 Stockport – Rehabilitation

Anna:

Eventually, Pete moved from Salford Royal Hospital to a rehabilitation centre in Stockport. I was absolutely horrified that the ward staff thought it appropriate to put Pete, unaccompanied, into a taxi for the transfer. He was so vulnerable, cognitively compromised, physically disabled and further weakened by the cancer treatment. To send him off with a taxi driver seemed irresponsible. Mum and Dad had been told to await his arrival by ambulance at the centre and they waited and waited until he eventually arrived by taxi!

The next day, his first at the rehab centre, Pete went by ambulance to another hospital for more scans. Shortly after that he started daily radiotherapy at The Christie Hospital. These treatments left him totally drained; weak and exhausted.

Pete was well enough eventually to start physiotherapy again and made great progress physically. He has always been a very physical person and a high achiever in physical endeavours. It played to his strengths to set goals and work towards achieving them. He worked hard but it was a difficult environment for him; a slow-paced rehab setting that was predominantly for older people. It was easier to visit though. Pete had his own room and it felt like a small step in the right direction.

I had a task to complete after my transfer to the neurological rehabilitation unit in Stockport – getting better! I arrived in a wheelchair, still unable to walk unsupported, and about to start a course of radiotherapy to complete my treatment for Hodgkin's Lymphoma which would drain me of energy and leave me feeling very weak again. Frustratingly, rehab had to go on hold. I would eventually leave 10 months later, thanking them for the stay and their hospitality!

I had dealt with chemotherapy. It felt like living through a bleak, Stella hangover (I was well-practised in dealing with those), but radiotherapy proved to be an altogether different beast. The first challenge was daily visits to The Christie for the radiotherapy sessions. The Hodgkin's Lymphoma was originally located in a lymph node in my neck. During each radiotherapy session a precise dose of radiation was delivered to that specific area. To achieve this, a plastic cast of my face was manufactured and at the commencement of each session the mask was placed over my face and 'bolted' down. Even if I'd wanted to move, I couldn't move a millimetre. While lying there, unable to twitch, my thoughts were immediately drawn to close friends who had lost their lives in avalanches ... if they had remained conscious, how terrifying their final few seconds would have been.

114

The location of the cancer resulted in my throat also catching the full intensity of the radiation. The soft tissues inside my throat were scorched and I was in a desperate degree of discomfort. One day, when I went into The Christie, the nurse pressed the emergency button on seeing how weak I was and I was escorted immediately to the treatment bay. The treatment routine persisted daily for three weeks and after each treatment I was good for nothing. I'd return to the rehabilitation centre and collapse into bed. All this proved too much for my then girlfriend who politely departed from the scene, leaving me to face a very uncertain future. Although Hodgkin's Lymphoma is commonly treatable, I knew that if the chemotherapy and radiotherapy failed, I'd be dead within 18 months. The events made me feel a white-hot rage. *"I'll show the bloody world. You've not seen the back of me!"* But first I needed sleep.

Val:

This was another very tough time for everyone. Bernie or I accompanied Pete for each of his fifteen sessions of radiotherapy and watched him become increasingly weak. This was all too much for his partner. She had been a wonderful support to Pete, spending as much time as possible with him throughout all his time in hospital but finally she felt she had to make the break. We worried that his fighting spirit might have finally abandoned him, but ...

Eventually I was ready to complete my task of getting better.

Years ago, I read an article about addiction and climbing. The article posed a list of questions such as:

Do you climb when you are injured?

Do you run yourself into debt to climb?

Do you lie to climb?

"Yes" to all of the above.

But climbing and exercise make me so happy, I just want more. Addicted to climbing, sport and life. There are far worse addictions to have. My secret to life was never getting bored, always wanting just a little bit more. This was not greed or gluttony but a hunger for achievement and success. This is the mindset of an athlete. I needed my next fix ... to walk alone outside, but that had been on hold whilst radiotherapy was in progress.

"Let's do this!" Radiotherapy had been completed, I was feeling better, now time to fight back again.

The Devonshire Centre for Neurorehabilitation was stripped down and minimalistic. However, it housed everything I needed: a gym and a bed. I have always written myself ambitious training plans. Regrettably, my ego is often bigger than my biceps and quadriceps put together. This was one plan I had to see through; learning to function again!

I showed my hand at the outset by wearing a Snowdon Marathon T-shirt in my first physio session. The physio enquired: *"Have you done that?"* *"Several times"* I replied. *"How long did you take?"* *"My best time is 3 hours 52 minutes."*

116

My physio was a runner too. From that moment we connected. He understood where I was mentally and what I wanted to achieve. It was under his instruction that I first used the centre's exercise bike. It took every ounce of energy I had to turn the pedals once. After one week of immense effort, I managed 100 metres. I was hooked!

Walking practice continued until one amazing day when, terrified, I emerged into the hazy, summer sunshine; not the alpine air I love so much but fresh air all the same. Most importantly, I was walking unaided at last!

Months later, plans for my discharge started. My dad and former partner had worked tirelessly, emptying and selling my house in Wales. Dad then set about helping me to sort out my future. I was allocated a social worker who did a great job. My sister Jane spotted a flat that suited me well, support workers were chosen, and I realised that I would finally be able to leave hospital.

Serendipity? Before I left the Devonshire Centre, Dad took me to visit Total Fitness in Wilmslow. He thought I might eventually enjoy the gym. How right he was! Total Fitness is a beautiful gym. It is one of the largest in Europe, complete with indoor running track, multiple swimming pools and every training aid / torture device the mind can imagine. Little did I know then the important and significant part this gym would play in my rehabilitation. It was here that I first met Rachel who was to become my physio when I eventually left hospital.

Over the Brink and Back

November 2014 – Home

Anna:

Nineteen months after the accident Pete was able to leave hospital and move into his own flat. He still required substantial support; he was mainly fed through a tube into his stomach overnight. This required 24-hour nursing care in the early days. However, this was reduced gradually, as was the domestic support that he needed to run the flat. The near-by gym became an important focus for Pete and complemented his rehab. He met a brilliant physio-turned-personal trainer, Rachel, who has been central to Pete's physical rehab. At last, he started to really regain fitness.

Training

After discharge from the Devonshire Centre into my own flat, I started regular sessions with Rachel. She is a person with tireless patience and endless optimism. She worked me out pretty quickly; laughed at my jokes, was always positive and fed me coffee with a spoonful of *very* soft chocolate (I still retained my PEG). I was putty in her hands. She made a real difference! The gym became my home from home as I attempted to regain fitness.

Following my success on the exercise bike at the rehabilitation centre, Dad researched cycling coaching with local organisations and suggested I try giving it a go. (Rachel also thought this a good idea.) He located a trainer, who worked with me and reacquainted me with cycling. My first attempt was at Stockport Wheelers on the Harriers' running track, used by a cycling club for people with disabilities. On my first visit I was put on an adult sized tricycle. I did two laps before requesting a 'normal' bike. The first 100m felt a bit shaky and very odd, but it's true – you never forget how to ride a bike!

Rachel then ran specific cycle training sessions for me on the gym tennis courts. I had to cycle round her whilst she held up different numbers of fingers. I had to shout out the number as I cycled. I undertook a series of her carefully thought-out exercises; it appeared to me that her level of input and creativity were well beyond that which a physio should be called upon to make. When she went on maternity leave, I was left in the capable hands of another physio who was desperately keen and competitive. She loved nothing more than working me to failure. I had to ease her concerns by explaining that it was quite normal for the veins in my forearms to look like a map of the London Underground! Under the care and direction of my two physios, I was again able to return to training in every waking hour.

Problems

However, there were still some obstacles to overcome. I hadn't eaten a morsel (except dissolved chocolate) for two years. A high-energy food mixture was pumped directly into my stomach via the PEG. This required a plastic tube that sat alongside my navel, permitting food to be pumped into my stomach overnight. Whilst being remotely fed I actually gained weight. This added insult to injury as I couldn't enjoy any of the food and I was gaining weight! I had built up quite an appetite after two years. My sleep was constantly disturbed by the whirring of the pump. It also impeded my early attempts at a few easy climbs; I decided that the possible consequences of my climbing harness disturbing the PEG tube to my stomach was not a price worth paying!

The news that my ability to swallow had recovered to a point where I could eat again was very welcome indeed, but I hadn't really considered the process or logistics of having the PEG removed. I was too excited about the prospect of being able to swim again. I presumed that it would involve a small cut, out it would come, and that would be that. It was only on arrival at hospital that I heard the plan; the surgical team would feed a camera and pincers down my throat, past my voice box and continue into my stomach. They would then locate the feeding end of the PEG and pull it back up my oesophagus, past my voice box again and remove it.

"Now, anaesthetic or sedative sir?" It sounded like such an unappealing decision to be forced into! I would much have preferred to hear *"Red or white sir? Can I recommend the '76 Chablis?"*. I declined their kind offer of a choice, instructing them to do their worst. What I

should have said was *"Both of the above!"* I like to imagine the process was like the famous scene in Jaws when they find a car registration plate in the shark's stomach. Finally though, I would be able to sleep, eat, climb, and swim again. The corollary was that I could indeed eat but it seemed that I might always have to have food softened or blended to avoid choking, another situation to be avoided.

Life still had not finished testing my resolve! A few months after returning home and resuming training again, I developed a deep vein thrombosis or DVT (a blood clot) in my arm, a complication of the treatment for Hodgkin's Lymphoma. This manifested itself in brutal pain and swelling in my whole arm. Neither were appreciated! I needed a daily injection of Fragmin, a substance used to thin my blood and help the clot to disperse. Medics warned *"If the clot were to move to your heart or brain, the results could be catastrophic"*. Luckily, it has, at times, been argued that I lack both …

The daily injections were administered beneath the skin of my abdomen, leaving it black and blue. I now lived in pain as my arm slowly recovered. The positive aspect of this situation was that I had previously been worried that my pain receptors may have been compromised because of the accident. They definitely had not! Unfortunately, I found myself in the doldrums. Climbing offered no appeal or sanctuary, and the nights were quickly drawing in and I was in great discomfort.

I binned the negatives, gathered my thoughts and assessed the situation. Considering my life graphically, the X axis should have finished at age 34, possibly 35. It was an absolute miracle that I had survived. A once in a lifetime alignment of the planets. I survived a stupidly big fall, I wasn't buried and I didn't drown. To top it all, the accident lead to the discovery of the cancer.

Come on man, damn well shake yourself. You've survived a 140 metre fall, pneumonia, sepsis, cancer and a DVT. You've won the EuroMillions! Are you really complaining because your arm hurts and the nights are drawing in? You must be the luckiest man alive.

I developed a mental trick whilst cycling. It worked amazingly well for me. Work in five-minute bouts. For three minutes work to exhaustion. If you can think of anything other than suppressing vomit you are not working hard enough. Recover for two minutes, then repeat the process. This distraction technique saw my plateau of recovery revert to an exponential curve.

Moving on

Kenneth Graham, author of The Wind in the Willows wrote some wonderful lines for his water rat character Ratty: *"Believe me, my young friend, there is nothing – absolutely nothing – half so much worth doing as simply messing about in boats."*

As my strength started to return, my mind began to wander … I really needed a project. I had tried some easy climbs with friends but, put in a situation where, after having once been the leader, I was now being 'looked after', I found that I took absolutely no pleasure in it. I loved cycling but I could do with resting my legs.

I had always had a love of the water. Kayaking and surfing were always the greatest threat to my climbing; not the ring ouzel, nor a multitude of other access problems to cliffs, but simply *water!* I would either have been found on a mountain or at the beach, a simple but wonderful way of life.

I got in touch with the team at Plas y Brenin to discuss the various possible projects I had in mind. It was agreed that kayaking would offer a much-needed rest for my legs and hopefully lead to being back on the sea. My first trip started in the canoe rolling pool. I'd had to learn to walk and talk again but after 15 years of kayaking, I was pleased to find I could still perform what is known as an Eskimo roll – the ability to right a capsized kayak. That movement was so hard-wired into my muscle memory, it would have required more than a rather long fall to forget it.

A plan was hatched to circumnavigate Anglesey by kayak when the days lengthened again. With help from Olly Sanders and Ben Lawes that journey quickly became reality. Admittedly, before we started, doubts began to gnaw at my thoughts. What if I couldn't even keep my balance in the kayak? In the early days of my recovery, I had tried to sit up in the hospital bed; I totally lost all balance and collapsed. That was the moment I understood the severity of my situation. It really is astonishing what we take for granted about our functioning until a malfunction occurs but, equally amazing, is what the body and specifically the brain can recover from. What if, what if, what if ... I thought, but what if it is well planned, well thought out and both Olly and Ben do a sterling job of reacquainting me with an old friend the sea? I interviewed myself without tea or biscuits and gave myself a stern talking to, I was ready to paddle!

We experienced blazing sun, howling winds and tropical deluges. Under the guidance of my expert companions, the trip became a reality and a huge success. Achievement really is fantastic; I craved more. Once is luck, twice a fluke but three times creates a pattern, reality. Training with Rachel at the gym, cycling and now kayaking. Things are really beginning to shape up!

Over the Brink and Back

Now

Rachel:

As Peter's physio I've had the privilege of helping a former athlete to re-kindle his fitness. I first met Pete at Total Fitness Gym, where I've now trained him for six years. It's hard to imagine that the man I first met would go on to achieve so much. At our initial meeting Pete had recently finished a course of chemotherapy and radiotherapy and his speech was barely comprehensible. He wore a hard hat, was scared of knocking into something and could barely walk ten metres without losing balance. We started cautiously, fully assessing Pete's ability. The nature of his injury had severely compromised his coordination and balance. Initially his movement around the gym floor was laboured and slow.

Pete has shown me many video clips and photos of his life pre-accident. It seems that climbing, mountaineering, surfing and skiing defined him. Although his injury has had an obvious and lasting legacy, his drive and determination remain intact. Pete always greets me with a smile and gives 100%. Only the other day he smiled and said "You simply don't fall 460 feet and get

127

away with it scot free. I'll either regain my fitness or die trying." He is an example of what drive and commitment can achieve, when faced with seemingly impossible odds. I look forward to seeing Pete go on to achieve everything he wants in life, and I feel privileged to be a part of that journey.

Anna:

So where are we now?

Pete continues to improve, even so many years after the accident. Progress is slower now; it's not linear either. Pete will seem to plateau and then will leap forwards again in terms of his ability. The impact of head injuries is so complex and so specific to the individual. I saw Pete last week and thought he had improved once again: his speech, his conversation, his ability to engage and to see other points of view.

There is no doubt that the accident was a dividing line in Pete's life, the magnitude of the injury and loss are immense. However, what is truly amazing is that, in the face of the greatest adversity, Pete remains motivated, cheerful and sees the opportunities that lie ahead of him. Pete cannot do everything that he could do before the accident, but he has his own home, a lovely girlfriend, he is as fit as a fiddle and he's happy. When I think back to the doctor's phrase, "may be able to communicate by blinking," it puts it all into perspective.

128

What does the future hold? None of us knows, but if this whole experience has taught us anything, it is not to underestimate Pete.

Val:

Hear, hear to everything Anna has said! Bernie and I are inspired by all that Pete has achieved and are incredibly proud of him. This is a great opportunity for our family to thank the huge number of people who have helped Pete since 12th April 2013: literally hundreds of people in five hospitals, support services in Stockport and good friends who have backed him all the way.

Over the Brink and Back

Finding Inner Peace

For the last nine years this has been my promised land.

For me the essence of life had been perpetual change and the excitement it brought. The change of the seasons dictated the discipline of choice.

January and the depths of winter meant ice climbing in Norway, winter climbing in Scotland, off-piste skiing in the European Alps and the occasional cold, clear day on the Derbyshire gritstone edges.

April indicated the end of the harsh, cold conditions and the commencement of ski mountaineering in the European Alps and ski touring on the high Norwegian plateaux. Also, time to get back in the ocean and surf and make the annual pilgrimage to Pembrokeshire to kick start the rock-climbing season.

June was all about trying to cram in as much rock climbing as I possibly could. Pretty much every night after teaching climbing all day, I could be found hanging off my local crag. If there was a swell on, I'd be down at the beach, surfing. These activities were enjoyed in double-time as I knew that June also indicated the start of another long alpine season, two and a half months of 00:00 alarm calls, scorching sun, magnificent views, terrifying lightning storms, constant danger and epically long days. I still tried to do two noteworthy alpine climbs for myself each summer. My last climb was a fitting conclusion to my alpine career; the Peuterey Integral, the longest and most committing ridge in the European Alps taking the alpinist from the valley floor, with over 4,500m of climbing, to the summit of Mont Blanc.

After two and a half months of Alpinism, there's no better way to unwind than to spend a week doing battle with the Atlantic swells on the west coast of France. Those long, sandy shore breakers just barrel their heads off. September, back in the UK, marks the start of the gritstone season. Cooler temperatures return to the Derbyshire edges, offering good friction on them again. It also heralds the arrival of the autumn storm swells. After work, I could be in the water at my local beach in 20 minutes.

My life was dictated by the weather. I'd spend any spare second scrutinising the latest barometric chart, trying to work out how best to play my chips. Any surplus time I had was spent volunteering with the local mountain rescue team.

Life was a perpetual smörgåsbord of excitement.

Now, who am I? A brain damaged, disabled, avalanche and cancer survivor.

How on earth has it come to this?

I'm disabled, I'm disabled ... Nooooo!

I absolutely hated the label of 'disabled'. To me, those words cut like glass. In Wales, I was known as Big Pete. Big Pete climbed, surfed, ran, took others up big mountains and in any spare time he had, he rescued people from them. There was an immense sense of loss, especially when I thought I would never walk or talk again. But I could so easily have lost everything, including my life, so in reality I won.

Eight years on, I have grown to almost relish the description 'disabled'.

I watched the Tokyo Olympics home-coming parade on television, a great event bursting with achievements by inspirational athletes. Behind every personal achievement there lies a story. For me, cycling the distance around the equator is the outcome of spending two years in five different hospitals across Europe, surviving cancer and learning to walk and talk again. There are many things in life I would have done differently but I genuinely feel I've given 101% to my rehabilitation and feel a real sense of achievement.

Initially, my mantra was; if you want to be a patient, accept being treated as a patient. I was not just a patient, and I found that the hardest loss to accept was that of my independence because I needed carers with me in my flat day and night. Although my mobility and voice lay in tatters, my inner strength from battling climbs, mountains and massive seas burned stronger than ever.

As an athlete, I was, perhaps, unexceptional. I climbed, ice climbed, skied, mountaineered, surfed and kayaked and now I cycle. I'm definitely a jack of all trades and master of none. Would I trade a wealth of global adventures, climbing in the Himalaya, European alpinism, skiing in the Alps and on the high Norwegian plateaux, surfing worldwide, kayaking on Norwegian rivers, rock climbing in America and Australia for the sole pursuit of a single discipline? Not a chance!

Growing up, my heroes were:

Jean-Marc Boivin, climber, extreme skier, diver, base jumper, and paraglider; Patrick Berhault, Mountain Guide, free climber, and skier; Ueli Steck, Mountain Guide, solo mountaineer, and all-round mountain athlete. These were extreme athletes who all pushed the limits of their sports, and all sadly died doing so.

Whilst enduring radiotherapy I remembered a very fitting quote that brought my situation into perspective: *"No matter how close to death you are, there's always someone closer."* My thoughts immediately turned to those colleagues and friends who had gone into the mountains and never returned. I remembered where I had been and what I was doing when I learned of their deaths ...

***

After another hard and exciting week of ski touring, we skied out from the Jotunheimen National Park. We'd enjoyed four days of remote storm-battered wilderness as we attempted to outflank the weather and scurry from hut to hut. The week had included an ascent of the remote and wild Galdhøpiggen, a respectable achievement in early Spring.

I quickly ran through the plan for the next few hours:

Return by coach to Sjusjøen (4 hours)

Return ski equipment to the stores, and clean and clear the accommodation (2 hours)

Travel to the airport (2 hours)

Catch flight to London

Transfer to flight to Manchester

Return to Wales (home)

I had a lot to accomplish that day.

I was catching my breath and boarding the London flight at Oslo airport when I received a phone call. *"Chris has been killed in an avalanche. He was descending from Buachaille Etive Mòr when a plaque of soft slab released."* A day of non-stop activity, in the middle of a bustling airport ... the world stood still.

Chris Walker was the life and soul of the climbing community, who he never failed to entertain. One of his anecdotes I've retold multiple times and is always met by laughter. Aged 16, Chris was fulfilling his work experience week at the local branch of Halfords. It was his first day and he was keen to impress. Suddenly the doors crashed open, and an armed gang ran in. Putting a sawn-off shotgun in Chris' face they demanded that he open the till. He politely and calmly responded that it was necessary to buy and scan an item to unlock the till.

Could he recommend a mint magic tree?

I still remember him telling the anecdote to an enthralled and amused crowd. Between pints they hung on his every word ...

***

The powder was so soft and light it formed a layer like champagne bubbles under my skis. Just one more turn, one more hit. I behaved like a junkie, as we disappeared deep into the trees, somewhere above La Grave (France). I hadn't seen any other ski tracks for ages and feared we were committing to a lobster pot (easy to get in, impossible to get out). Andy Nelson and I came to a crashing halt as the reality of our situation became apparent. We'd inadvertently skied right onto the top of La Pylon a popular 80 metre ice fall. We stood on a mixture of water ice and hard frozen snow. We didn't dare sneeze!

Slowly, slowly, and very carefully we took off our skis and started the relentless, uphill plodding through waist deep snow. Hours later we staggered into the village of La Grave. *"I need caffeine and sugar!"* I announced as we walked through the narrow, winter-bound streets. We returned to the flat to meet the other members of our group and help prepare the communal meal.

The post-activity scene in the flat was very similar to a post-heist sequence in a gangster movie. Many hands chip in, as a culinary masterpiece is created. Steamy bodies clothed in a collection of thermals, fleeces and brightly coloured ski pants work in harmony like would-be chefs in an episode of Master Chef. Personally, at Spanish omelette production, involving peeling and slicing and dicing, I'm as good as you'll find. But that's where it ends!

A group member slips out of the meal to take a phone call. He returns and beckons me over. *"Rupert Rosedale has been killed in an avalanche on Ben Nevis!"*

There's that hollow feeling again. Epic ski descents, the hustle and bustle of post activity debriefs and a busy evening of team cooking, then ... the immense sadness that another friend has left the party.

* * *

Probability. What a desperately cruel mistress. The problem is, the more you court and dice with death, the more you're suckered into believing in your own invincibility. As far as I was concerned, I was the invincible Achilles, a demi-god of the mountains, that is, until the wheels fell off in quite a dramatic fashion. As a climber, skier, surfer and mountaineer, I lived my life by a single mantra: *"Go big or go home"*. I went home!

Every year at the British Mountain Guides' annual general meeting, we held a minutes silence for those killed in the mountains.

It is with great relief that I appear to be approaching my promised land. My latest challenges include cycling around France, Majorca, Spain and Switzerland and cycling the equivalent distance to that of the circumference of the equator (41,075 km), with the equivalent height gain of 43 ascents of Everest since leaving hospital. These were thoroughly enjoyable, a productive use of time and a means of gaining and maintaining physical fitness.

Wind the clock back nine years, my parents flanked me as I stumbled through Woodbank Park on the way to the Stockport Harriers running track and a Stockport Wheelers meet, the local disabled cycling club. On my first visit I was put on a trike and happy with my completion of one lap.

I was cycling the other day and stopped at my favourite café. While enjoying a cup of tea I fell into conversation with two other cyclists. One looked confused and said, *"You don't sound like you're from round here."* I then explained that my speech was the result of an accident and showed him a photo on my phone of me on life support. They were both amazed that anyone could survive a140 metre fall and such an extensive list of medical problems and complications. One of the cyclists was a stroke survivor and could fully understand the frustration of learning to talk again.

And so, nine years on, what battle scars do I carry? I've got a slight depression on the right side of my skull where I hit the rock and subsequently had surgery, a faint Harry Potter scar above my left eye, where I hit another rock, and my gait is very odd, so walking doesn't come easily. Despite cycling the equivalent to the distance around the equator, 12km remains my longest walk to date. There's also a deep scar over my Adam's apple, where I was ventilated and I now have a second belly button, where the feeding tube was inserted.

My issues now fluctuate between an inconvenience and a problem, and I live with the constant threat of choking, so food has to be blended. My love of food has totally gone, and I just see food as fuel. I used to love the wide variety of tastes and textures food would provide. I've never had any time or patience for fussy eating, but if I were to choke, I could be dead in three minutes. The logistics of a battered swallow are a massive inconvenience. I'm currently laying plans for a bike-packing trip round the country. I have to plan this carefully; to buy, make and check the consistency of every dehydrated meal before I go. Usually, I blend the life out of everything. My favourite food used to be 'blue' steak and peppercorn sauce. It's now tiramisu and coffee!

The initial frustration of not being able to talk clearly has eased somewhat, though it does create some problems. I would say my voice has now become a part of my identity. I do, however, deliberately avoid phone conversations and favour text. My speech is slurred and sounds like I'm drunk, despite being teetotal for more than eight years. People recoil initially but usually quickly adjust on listening carefully to my words. When meeting people for the first time I quickly apologise for my slurred speech which helps put people at ease. I still have a speech therapist.

Big bloody Ben. In hospital the speech therapist would request, encourage, cajole or demand that I narrated a piece of writing about Big Ben. In the hospital ward I'd talk about its 9ft hands and how its name originates from the bell it houses. At the time I was fully aware of my prognosis: *"In time, Pete might be able to blink to communicate"*.

"Life is so good, I can taste it in my spit" Daniel Craig, Layer Cake 2004; a beautifully graphic description of enjoyment, a description I've referred to many times in my mountain career. Everyone can relate to life's highs and lows. Highs now stand out in technicolour and are amazingly lucid. After almost completely losing my memory, it has slowly returned ... a slow trickle at first. It took me a year before I could remember my age. The trickle then grew to a torrent. An abundance of memories flooded back, but only happy, positive memories returned. I have a detailed archive of every great climb I have done, but my only memory of real hardship is the descent from the Aiguille Noir, 10 hours of loose, dangerous, dehydrated hell. I would describe myself as an optimistic person. I've never been a realist, but definitely an optimist. A symptom of optimism is the total failure to recall negative memories. My short-term memory is no longer automatic and if I'm going to successfully remember a detail, I have to make an effort to positively remember it as it occurs. Consequently, I rely heavily on systems and procedures. As we all leave the house, I'm sure we check for wallet, keys, phone. This is now what I do for every important detail of everyday life.

As a result of the traumatic brain injury, I have at long last developed an abundance of emotion. This is caused by damage deep inside the limbic system, a system that regulates one's emotions. I'm sure we can all think of a situation where laughter would be an appalling outcome. Somehow, for me, the consequence of the action seems to heighten the apparent humour of the situation. Well, now I don't laugh. I absolutely roar. I laugh until tears roll down my cheeks and the act of laughter physically exhausts me. After minutes that feel like hours of laughter, I let out a sigh of exhaustion and regain composure. In contrast, and being a bloke, far harder to accept, I now seem to get upset more easily. I was talking to my friend Rachel about the details of the accident and started crying. Seeing me in apparent distress, she started crying too! I had to give myself a stern talking to and an interview without tea or biscuits before I was once again collected.

The human soul is very like a car fuel tank. You quickly glance at the dashboard, and to your horror realise you're almost empty. You hold your breath and remember that there's a garage in 20 miles. At this point the warning light comes on. You're now running on fumes and fresh air but somehow the car creeps on. Under extreme stress, the soul sometimes seems able to access reserves you never knew you had: reserves of hope, optimism, humour and fortitude. My message to anyone who suffers with their mental health is that below the surface, they will have strength they never knew existed. It's not physical strength and doesn't require a loaded bench press to quantify it but, be assured it's there, though help might be needed to find it.

My recovery has, according to clinicians, been surprising and remarkable, and once again opened up a world of limitless opportunities. In fact, at the tender age of 43 I should perhaps be thinking about retiring, but instead I now face new challenges and obstacles and can achieve success all over again, this time as a brain-damaged athlete.

See you in the mountains!

Addendum

Anna:

Pete asked mum and I to write some thoughts, giving a perspective from the family to accompany his account of his accident and rehab. It felt a bit overwhelming, and I did not really know where to start. I decided to detail a few stand out memories; this is by no means an exhaustive account ... possibly not even completely accurate. You will appreciate that it was a difficult time; we travelled lots, slept little and worried incessantly, none of which lends itself to historical accuracy. It is also several years ago now and the impact of this alone is significant and we often find that, even within the family, we remember things differently.

A Note from the Author

As you shiver your way through cold bivouacs, are cooked by the mid-summer heat or battered by cruel winter storms remember this. Time is linear, you'll never pass by this way again.